Law Today

Richard Powell

Longman

Contents

	Introduction	6
	Law: A necessary evil?	
	Scope of this book	

Part One: General Issues
1	**What is law?**	9
	Descriptive and prescriptive	
	Social morality, rules and laws	
2	**Sources of modern law**	14
	Historical and political background	
	Common law systems	
	Continental systems	
	Modern Japanese law	
	Socialist legal systems	
3	**Civil and public law**	21
	Main categories	
	Differences in procedure	
	Points of contact	
4	**Judicial institutions**	25
	English courts	
	International comparisons	
	Appeals	
	Lower courts	
	Restrictions	
5	**Lawyers at work**	31
	Professional titles	
	Range of work	
	Entering the profession	
	Regulating the profession	
	Legalese	

Part Two: Legal Principles
6	**Contracts**	38
	Different types	
	Essential elements	
	Damages	
	Other remedies	

7	**Criminal Law**	45
	What is a crime?	
	Elements of proof	
	Defenses	
8	**Torts**	51
	Comparison with crimes	
	Comparison with broken contracts	
	Requirements of proof	
9	**Trusts**	57
	Different types	
	Enforcers and administrators	
	Requirements	
10	**Land law**	61
	Complexity	
	Estate in English law	
	Legal interests	
	Land transfer	
	Short-term possession	
	Regulation of private and public land	

Part Three: The Law in Practice

11	**Running a business**	68
	Organization	
	Internal management	
	Termination	
12	**The law and the family**	75
	Marriage law	
	Divorce law	
	Protection of children	
	Rights of succession	
13	**The law and consumers**	82
	Contracts	
	Exemptions	
	Product liability	
14	**Employment law**	88
	Employment rights	
	EC employment law	
	Comparison with Japan	
15	**Intellectual property**	93
	Patents and copyrights	

    Keeping pace with technology
    Trademarks and trade secrets

Part Four: Law, Politics and Society

16 **Freedom of speech and expression**   97
    Political censorship
    Words of violence and racism
    Art, literature and pornography
    Defamation

17 **The rights of citizens**   104
    Constitutional law
    Separation of powers
    Rights of citizens

18 **Human rights**   109
    Law and politics
    Cultural differences
    International agreements
    Human rights violations
    Racial and sexual discrimination

19 **Enforcing the law**   115
    Role of police force
    Civil and criminal penalties
    Capital punishment

20 **Internationalization of the law**   121
    Growth of international law
    Conflicts of national sovereignty
    Internationalizing legal systems

Glossary   127

Introduction

Law: a necessary evil?

In the opinion of many people, the law is a necessary evil that should be used only when everyday, informal ways of settling disputes break down. When we buy a train ticket a lawyer may tell us it represents a contract with legal obligations, but to most of us it is just a ticket that gets us on the train. If our neighbor plays loud music late at night, we probably try to discuss the matter with him rather than consulting the police, lawyers or the courts. Only when we are injured in a train accident, or when a neighbor refuses to behave reasonably, do we start thinking about the legal implications of everyday activities.

Even so, some transactions in modern society are so complex that few of us would risk making them without first seeking legal advice; for example, buying or selling a house, setting up a business, or deciding whom to give our property to when we die. In some societies, such as the United States, precise written contracts, lawyers and courts of law have become a part of daily life, whereas in others, such as Japan, lawyers are few and people tend to rely on informal ways of solving disagreements. It is interesting that two highly industrialized societies should be so different in this respect.

On the whole it seems that people all over the world are becoming more and more accustomed to using legal means to regulate their relations with each other. Multinational companies employ expensive experts to ensure that their contracts are valid wherever they do business. Non-industrialized tribes in South America use lawyers in order to try to stop governments from destroying the rainforests in which they live. In the former Soviet republics where law was long regarded as merely a function of political power, ordinary citizens nowadays challenge the decisions of their governments in courts of law. And at a time when workers, refugees, commodities and environmental pollution are traveling around the world faster than ever before, there are increasing attempts to internationalize legal standards. When it helps ordinary people to reach just agreements across social, economic and international barriers, law seems to be regarded as a good thing. However, when it involves time and money and highlights people's inability to cooperate informally, law seems to be an evil—but a necessary one that everyone should have a basic knowledge of.

Scope of this book

The purpose of this book is to give students a general introduction to the law, whether or not they intend to specialize in legal studies. Despite greater internationalization, most law is still made and enforced by individual governments, and there are great differences among the world's systems of law. For much of this book, English law has been chosen as a model. But frequent comparisons have been made with the principles and institutions of other parts of the world, especially with the United States, whose legal system closely resembles that of England, and with Western Europe and Japan.

The book is divided into four parts. The first five chapters deal with some general issues: what law is, where it comes from and the legal traditions that have developed in different parts of the world; the division between civil and public law, the institutions in which laws are made and applied, and the work of lawyers themselves.

The next five chapters are concerned with some important legal principles: contracts, crimes, torts, trusts and land law. Most areas of legal work employ some of these principles, so it is useful to have some knowledge of them before looking at how the law is applied in practice.

The next five chapters consider the role of law in regulating some areas of economic and social life: running a business, consuming products and services, family life, employment, and intellectual property (inventions, designs, copyrights).

The final five chapters take a look at some wide topics where legal developments are closely related to social and political ones: freedom of speech and expression, citizens' rights, human rights, law enforcement, and the internationalization of the law.

A glossary of the key legal terms used in this book is provided for reference at the end of the book.

The words which occur in bold in the text are key concepts for that chapter, and are then defined. Some of them are also in the glossary.

Exercises

Comprehension
1 In what circumstances do people think of their everyday activities as legal matters?
2 Which statement(s) is/are true?
 a Japanese prefer written agreements to informal ones.
 b There are more lawyers in the United States than in Japan.
 c Contracts and courts of law are a part of ordinary people's daily life in all industrialized countries.
3 Give examples of the growing uses of law throughout the world.

Discussion
"Society can do without lawyers."
Write a paragraph containing two arguments for and two against this statement. Then discuss your answer with other students.

Part One
General Issues

1 What is law?

Descriptive and prescriptive

The English word "law" refers to limits upon various forms of behavior. Some laws are descriptive: they simply describe how people, or even natural phenomena, usually behave. An example is the rather consistent law of gravity; another is the less consistent laws of economics. Other laws are prescriptive—they prescribe how people ought to behave. For example, the speed limits imposed upon drivers are laws that prescribe how fast we should drive. They rarely describe how fast we actually do drive, of course. This book is concerned with certain kinds of prescriptive law.

Social morality, rules and laws

In all societies, relations between people are regulated by prescriptive laws. Some of them are customs—that is, informal rules of social and moral behavior. Some are rules we accept if we belong to particular social institutions, such as religious, educational and cultural groups. And some are precise laws made by nations and enforced against all citizens within their power. This book is mainly concerned with the last kind of law, and it is important to consider to what extent such laws can be distinguished from customs and social rules.

Customs need not be made by governments, and they need not be written down. We learn how we are expected to behave in society through the instruction of family and teachers, the advice of friends, and our experiences in dealing with strangers. Sometimes, we can break these rules without suffering any penalty. But if we continually break the rules, or break a very important one, other members of society may ridicule us, criticize us, act violently toward us or refuse to have anything to do with us. The ways in which people talk, eat and drink, work, and relax together are usually guided by many such informal rules which have very little to do with laws created by governments.

The rules of social institutions tend to be more formal than customs, carrying precise penalties for those who break them. They are not, however, enforceable by any political authority. Sports clubs, for example, often have detailed rules for their members. But if a member breaks a rule and refuses to accept any punishment, the club may have no power other than to ask him or her to leave the club.

However, when governments make laws for their citizens, they use a system of courts backed by the power of the police to enforce these laws. Of course, there may be instances where the law is not enforced against someone—such as when young children commit crimes, when the police have to concentrate on certain crimes and therefore ignore others, or in countries where there is so much political corruption that certain people are able to escape justice by using their money or influence. But the general nature of the law considered in this book is that it is enforced equally against all members of the nation.

Government-made laws are nevertheless often patterned upon informal rules of conduct already existing in society, and relations between people are regulated by a combination of all these rules. This relationship can be demonstrated using the example of a sports club.

Suppose a member of a rugby club is so angry with the referee during a club game that he hits him and breaks his nose. At the most informal level of social custom, it is probable that people seeing or hearing about the incident would criticize the player and try to persuade him to apologize and perhaps compensate the referee in some way. At a more formal level, the player would find he had broken the rules of his club, and perhaps of a wider institution governing the conduct of all people playing rugby, and would face punishment, such as a fine or a suspension before he would be allowed to play another game. Finally, the player might also face prosecution for attacking the referee under laws created by the government of his country. In many countries there might be two kinds of prosecution. First, the referee could conduct a civil action against the player, demanding compensation for his injury and getting his claim enforced by a court of law if the player failed to agree privately. Second, the police might also start an action against the player for a crime of violence. If found guilty, the player might be sent to prison, or he might be made to pay a fine to the court—that is, punishment for an offence against the state, since governments often consider anti-social behavior not simply as a matter between two individuals but as a danger to the well-being and order of society as a whole.

What motives do governments have in making and enforcing laws? Social control is undoubtedly one purpose. Public laws establish the authority of the government itself, and civil laws provide a framework for interaction among citizens. Without laws, it is argued, there would be anarchy in society (although anarchists themselves argue that human beings would be able to interact peacefully without laws if there were no governments to interfere in our lives).

Another purpose is the implementation of justice. Justice is a concept that most people feel is very important but few are able to define. Sometimes a just decision is simply a decision that most people feel is fair. But will we create a just society by simply observing public opinion? If we are always fair to majorities, we will often be unfair to minorities. If we do what seems to be fair at the moment, we may create unfairness in the future. What should the court decide, for example, when a man kills his wife because she has a painful illness and begs him to help her die? It seems unjust to find him guilty of a crime, yet if we do not, isn't there a danger that such mercy-killing will become so widespread that abuses will occur? Many philosophers have proposed concepts of justice that are much more theoretical than everyday notions of fairness. And sometimes governments are influenced by philosophers, such as the French revolutionaries who tried to implement Montesquieu's doctrine of the Separation of Powers (Chapter 17); or the Russian revolutionaries who accepted Marx's assertion that systems of law exist to protect the property of those who have political power. But in general, governments are guided by more practical considerations such as rising crime rates or the lobbying of pressure groups.

Sometimes laws are simply an attempt to implement common sense. It is obvious to most people that dangerous driving should be punished; that fathers should provide financial support for their children if they desert their families; that a person should be compensated for losses when someone else breaks an agreement with him or her. But in order to be enforced, common sense needs to be defined in law, and when definitions are being written, it becomes clear that common sense is not such a simple matter. Instead, it is a complex skill based upon long observation of many different people in different situations. Laws based upon common sense don't necessarily look much like common sense when they have been put into words!

In practice, governments are neither institutions solely interested in retaining power, nor clear-thinking bodies implementing justice and common sense. They combine many purposes and inherit many traditions. The laws that they make and enforce reflect this confusion.

The laws made by the government of one country are often very different from the laws of another country. This makes it difficult to write a general introductory book about the law today. A book about economics, for example, while mentioning different practices and aims in different parts of the world, can focus upon those aspects of economics common to most parts of the modern world. But although there is a growing body of international law—and this will be dealt with as the final chapter of the book—the law today is, to a large extent, a complex of different and relatively independent national systems.

Most of the examples in this book come from English law. Despite major revisions over the centuries, the legal system of England and Wales is one of the oldest still operating in the modern world. (Scotland and Northern Ireland have their own internal legal systems, although many laws made by the British government operate throughout Britain.) English law has directly influenced the law of former British colonies such as Australia, India, Canada and the nation where law plays a bigger part in everyday life than anywhere else, the United States. In the following chapters these countries will be referred to frequently. In addition, although the legal systems of Western Europe and Japan come from rather different traditions, there are enough similarities of principle and institution to make comparison useful here, too.

Exercises

Comprehension
1 Give your own example of a descriptive law and a prescriptive law.
2 Which is/are true?
   a Social customs and rules are both enforced by governments.
   b Many laws reflect social customs.
   c Unlike social customs, laws are usually international.
3 Name four possible influences on a government when it is making a law.
4 Why do some laws appear to differ from common sense?

Discussion
"Mercy killing should not be punished."
Write a paragraph containing two points for and two against this statement. Then discuss your answer with other students.

2 Sources of modern law

Historical and political background

In order to understand why a particular country has a particular legal system, it is necessary to look at its history, political structure and social values. When there is political and social upheaval, one of the main concerns of a new government is to revise the legal system. Britain has had an unusual degree of political continuity. Despite civil wars in the fifteenth and seventeenth centuries and enormous social changes associated with industrialization, England and Wales have retained many laws and legal principles that originated eight centuries ago. On the other hand, most of the law of Japan, which experienced the rapid upheaval of the Meiji Restoration and foreign occupation after the Second World War, was developed within the last century.

Each country in the world, even each state of the United States, has its own system of law. However, for the purposes of this book it is generally true to say that there are two main traditions of law in the world. One is based on English **Common law**, and has been adopted by many Commonwealth countries and most of the United States. The other tradition, sometimes known as **Continental**, or **Roman law**, has developed in most of continental Europe, Latin America and many countries in Asia and Africa which have been strongly influenced by Europe. Continental law has also influenced Japan and several socialist countries.

Common law systems

Common law, or case law systems, particularly that of England, differ from Continental law in having developed gradually throughout history, not as the result of government attempts to define or codify every legal relation. Customs and court rulings have been as important as statutes (government legislation). Judges do not merely apply the law, in some cases they make law, since their interpretations may become precedents for other courts to follow.

Before William of Normandy invaded England in 1066, law was administered by a series of local courts and no law was common to the whole kingdom. The Norman Kings sent traveling judges around the country and gradually a "common law" developed, under the authority of three common law courts in London. Judges dealt with both criminal cases and civil disputes between individuals. Although local and ancient customs played their part, uniform application of the law throughout the country was promoted by the gradual development of the **doctrine of precedent**.

By this principle, judges attempted to apply existing customs and laws to each new case, rather than looking to the government to write new laws. If the essential elements of a case were the same as those of previous recorded cases, then the judge was bound to reach the same decision regarding guilt or innocence. If no precedent could be found, then the judge made a decision based upon existing legal principles, and his decision would become a precedent for other courts to follow when a similar case arose. The doctrine of precedent is still a central feature of modern common law systems. Courts are bound by the decisions of previous courts unless it can be shown that the facts differ from previous cases. Sometimes governments make new laws—statutes—to modify or clarify the common law, or to make rules where none existed before. But even statutes often need to be interrupted by the courts in order to fit particular cases, and these interpretations become new precedents. In common law systems, the law is, thus, found not only in government statutes, but also in the historical records of cases.

Another important feature of the common law tradition is **equity**. By the fourteenth century many people in England were dissatisfied with the inflexibility of the common law, and a practice developed of appealing directly to the king or to his chief legal administrator, the lord chancellor. As the lord chancellor's court became more willing to modify existing common law in order to solve disputes; a new system of law developed alongside the common law. This system recognized rights that were not enforced as common law but which were considered "equitable," or just, such as the right to force someone to fulfill a contract rather than simply pay damages for breaking it (see specific performance, Chapter 6), or the rights of a beneficiary of a trust (see Chapter 9). The courts of common law and of equity existed alongside each other for centuries. If an equitable principle would bring a different result from a common law ruling on the same case, then the general rule was that equity should prevail.

One problem resulting from the existence of two systems of justice was that a person often had to begin actions in different courts in order to get a satisfactory solution. For example, in a breach (breaking) of contract claim, a person had to seek **specific performance** (an order forcing the other party to do something) in court of equity, and damages (monetary compensation for his loss) in a common law court. In 1873, the two systems were unified, and nowadays a lawyer can pursue common law and equitable claims in the same court.

Although courts continually have to find ways of interpreting existing common law for new cases, legislation has become the most important source of new law. When the government feels that existing common law, equity, or statutes are in need of revision or clarification, it passes new legislation. In this way courts avoid the obligation to follow precedent. Parliament passes hundreds of new laws every year on matters that need to be regulated more precisely than the common law has been able to do and on matters that never arose when the common law was developed. For example, modern society has produced crimes such as business fraud and computer theft which require complex and precise definitions. Some modern legislation is so precise and comprehensive it is rather like a code in the Continental system.

The spread of common law in the world is due both to the once widespread influence of Britain in the world and the growth of its former colony, the United States. Although judges in one common law country cannot directly support their decisions by cases from another, it is permissible for a judge to note such evidence in giving an explanation. Nevertheless, political divergence has produced legal divergence from England. Unified federal law is only a small part of American law. Most of it is produced by individual states and reflects various traditions. The state of Louisiana, for example, has a Roman civil form of law which derives from its days as a French colony. California has a case law tradition, but its laws are codified as extensively as many Continental systems. Quebec is an island of French law in the Canadian sea of case law. In India, English common law has been codified and adopted alongside a Hindu tradition of law. Sri Lanka has inherited a criminal code from the Russian law introduced by the Dutch, and an uncodified civil law introduced by the British.

Continental systems

Continental systems are sometimes known as codified legal systems. They have resulted from attempts by governments to produce a set of codes to govern every legal aspect of a citizen's life. Thus it was necessary for the legislators to speculate quite comprehensively about human behavior rather than simply looking at previous cases. In codifying their legal systems, many countries have looked to the examples of Revolutionary and Napoleonic France, whose legislators wanted to break with previous case law, which had often produced corrupt and biased judgments, and to apply new egalitarian social theories to the law. Nineteenth century

Sources of modern law

Figure 2.1 *A lawyer at work in Sri Lanka, one of the countries with a common law system.*

Europe also saw the decline of several multi-ethnic empires and the rise of nationalism. The lawmakers of new nations sometimes wanted to show that the legal rights of their citizens originated in the state, not in local customs, and thus it was the state that was to make law, not the courts. In order to separate the roles of the legislature and judiciary, it was necessary to make laws that were clear and comprehensive. The lawmakers were often influenced by the model of the canon law of the Roman Catholic Church, but the most important models were the codes produced in the seventh century under the direction of the Roman Emperor Justinian. His aim had been to eliminate the confusion of centuries of inconsistent lawmaking by formulating a comprehensive system that would entirely replace existing law. Versions of Roman law had long influenced many parts of Europe, including the case law traditions of Scotland, but had little impact on English law.

It is important not to exaggerate the differences between these two traditions of law. For one thing, many case law systems, such as California's, have areas of law that have been comprehensively codified. For another, many countries can be said to have belonged to the Roman tradition long before codifying their laws, and large uncodified—perhaps uncodifiable—areas of the law still remain. French public law has never been codified, and French courts have produced a great deal of case law in interpreting codes that become out of date because of social change. The clear distinction between legislature and judiciary has weakened in many countries, including Germany, France and Italy, where courts are able to challenge the constitutional legality of a law made by parliament (see **judicial review**, Chapter 17).

Despite this, it is also important not to exaggerate similarities among systems within the Continental tradition. For example, while adopting some French ideas, such as separation of the legislature and judiciary, the late nineteenth century codifiers of German law aimed at conserving customs and traditions peculiar to German history. Canon law had a stronger influence in countries with a less secular ideology than France, such as Spain.

Modern Japanese law

Despite a tradition of private law that more closely resembled English principles of judicial precedent, the lawmakers of Meiji Japan decided to adopt criminal and civil codes closely based on the existing French models. However, this rapid import of a new system was to a large extent an attempt to give Japan the appearance of a modernized, even Westernized country, and the way in which justice was actually administered continued to reflect older Japanese principles of refraining wherever possible from formal and open methods of solving disputes. New codes of law developed under the postwar occupation show some influence from Anglo-American common law traditions (such as a statutory form of trust).

Socialist legal systems

According to classical Marxism, legal systems in capitalist and pre-capitalist nations were created to reinforce and justify property relations. Legal relations should not be thought of as in any way independent from political relations, which are based on ownership of property. In other words, the law is on the side of those with economic power. Marx theorized that with the coming of socialism, the state, and thus a state-produced system of law, would become irrelevant to social relations and would disappear.

However, socialist countries in the twentieth century have produced very strong centralized state institutions and complex legal systems alongside them. The leaders of the Soviet Revolution, and hence the governments of many nations that came under Soviet influence, tried to apply socialist ideology to a Continental civil law tradition in as systematic and comprehensive a way as possible. This ideology is clearly stated, and socialist lawmakers criticized both common law and previous Roman civil law systems for masking their own capitalist ideology in apparently neutral, unbiased institutions. In China, law courts are still primarily regarded as political instruments, used both to control theft and violence (still sometimes referred to in China as the remains of the class struggle) and to deal with political opponents. But recently, citizens in some areas have been encouraged to seek legal redress in disputes with other citizens, for example over consumer matters. Attempts have been made to codify Chinese law comprehensively, but so far there has been little progress. Even before the rejection of their socialist traditions, the Soviet republics had started to allow an increase in civil law cases, and a long process of revising existing civil and criminal codes had begun. As separatist movements grew in many parts of the Soviet Union, there was also development in Constitutional law, with some republics questioning the legality, both in Soviet and local law, of their obligations to the central government.

Sources of modern law

Exercises

Comprehension

1. Explain the doctrine of "precedent."
2. Which is/are true?
   a. Both California and Louisiana have continental systems of law.
   b. Most of Canada and the U.S. have common law.
   c. Louisiana and Quebec share some legal traditions.
3. How do Continental systems usually differ from common law systems?
4. Why does Japanese law include both common law and Continental law influences?
5. What changes have been taking place in Chinese law?

Discussion

"The main purpose of law is to protect property ownership."

Write a paragraph containing two arguments for and two against this statement. Then discuss your answer with other students.

3   Civil and public law

Main categories

One important distinction made in all these countries is between private—or civil—law and public law. **Civil** law concerns disputes among citizens within a country, and **public** law concerns disputes between citizens and the state, or between one state and another. The main categories of English civil law are:

Contracts: binding agreements between people (or companies);
Torts: wrongs committed by one individual against another individual's person, property or reputation;
Trusts: arrangements whereby a person administers property for another person's benefit rather than his own Land Law;
Probate: arrangements for dealing with property after the owner's death;
Family Law.

The main categories of public law are:

Crimes: wrongs which, even when committed against an individual are considered to harm the well-being of society in general;
Constitutional Law: regulation of how the law itself operates and of the relation between private citizen and government;
International Law: regulation of relations between governments and also between private citizens of one country and those of another.

In codified systems there are codes that correspond to these categories, for example, France's Code Civil and Code Pénal. Justinian's Roman codes covered such areas of law as contracts, property, inheritance, torts, the family, unjust enrichment, the law of persons, and legal remedies, but said little about criminal law. Consequently, most Continental criminal codes are entirely modern inventions.

Differences in procedure

Most countries make a rather clear distinction between civil and criminal procedures. For example, an English criminal court may force a defendant to pay a fine as punishment for his crime, and he may sometimes have to pay the legal costs of the prosecution. But the victim of the crime pursues his claim for compensation in a civil, not a criminal, action. (In France, however, a victim of a crime may be awarded damages by a criminal court judge.)

The standards of proof are higher in a criminal action than in a civil one since the loser risks not only financial penalties but also being sent to prison (or, in some countries, executed). In English law the prosecution must prove the guilt of a criminal "beyond reasonable doubt"; but the plaintiff in a civil action is required to prove his case "on the balance of probabilities." Thus, in a civil case a crime cannot be proven if the person or persons judging it doubt the guilt of the suspect and have a reason (not just a feeling or intuition) for this doubt. But in a civil case, the court will weigh all the evidence and decide what is most probable.

Criminal and civil procedure are different. Although some systems, including the English, allow a private citizen to bring a criminal prosecution against another citizen, criminal actions are nearly always started by the state. Civil actions, on the other hand, are usually started by individuals.

Some courts, such as the English Magistrates Courts (see Chapter 4) and the Japanese Family Court, deal with both civil and criminal matters. Others, such as the English Crown Court, deal exclusively with one or the other.

In Anglo-American law, the party bringing a criminal action (that is, in most cases, the state) is called the **prosecution**, but the party bringing a civil action is the **plaintiff**. In both kinds of action the other party is known as the **defendant**. A criminal case against a person called Ms. Sanchez would be described as "The People vs. (= versus, or against) Sanchez" in the United States and "R. (Regina, that is, the Queen) vs. Sanchez" in England. But a civil action between Ms. Sanchez and a Mr. Smith would be "Sanchez vs. Smith" if it was started by Sanchez, and "Smith vs. Sanchez" if it was started by Mr. Smith.

Evidence from a criminal trial is not necessarily admissable as evidence in a civil action about the same matter. For example, the victim of a road accident does not directly benefit if the driver who injured him is found guilty of the crime of careless driving. He still has to prove his case in a civil action. In fact he may be able to prove his civil case even when the driver is found not guilty in the criminal trial.

Once the plaintiff has shown that the defendant is liable, the main argument in a civil court is about the amount of money, or **damages**, which the defendant should pay to the plaintiff.

Points of contact

Nevertheless there are many point of contact between criminal and civil law. In most countries if the loser of a civil case refuses to comply with the order made against him—for example, to pay money to the winner of the action—the procedures for forcing him to comply may result in a criminal prosecution. Disobeying any court may constitute criminal conduct, and the disobedient loser of a civil action may find he or she not only has to pay the damages originally ordered by the court, but a criminal penalty as well.

Although the guilty defendant in a criminal case will not automatically be found liable in a civil action about the same matter, his chances of avoiding civil liability are not good. This is because the standard of proof in the civil case is lower than it was in the criminal case. The plaintiff will therefore make sure any information about a relevant criminal case is passed to the civil court.

It is also possible in English law to bring a civil action against the police. Sometimes this is done by someone who was mistreated when questioned by the police about a criminal case. This right, along with the right to challenge government decisions in courts of law, is discussed in Chapter 14.

Civil and public law

Exercises

Comprehension
1 In English law an act of violence against a person may be treated both as a crime and as a civil tort. Explain some of the differences between the two procedures.
2 Compare the principles of "proof beyond reasonable doubt" and "proof on the balance of probabilities."
3 Which is/are true?
 a Both damages and fines are sums of money.
 b Both damages and fines may benefit the victim of an accident.
 c Damages are part of the civil system of law.

Task
Try to draw a plan of the court system in your country, showing which courts have civil functions and which have criminal functions. Compare your plan with another student's. Use a dictionary to check the English names of the different types of courts.

4 Judicial institutions

In all legal systems there are institutions for creating, modifying, abolishing and applying the law. Usually these take the form of a hierarchy of courts. The role of each court and its capacity to make decisions is strictly defined in relation to other courts. There are two main reasons for having a variety of courts. One is that a particular court can specialize in particular kinds of legal actions—for example, family courts and juvenile courts. The other is so that a person who feels his case was not fairly treated in a lower court can appeal to a higher court for reassessment (although the right of **appeal** usually depends upon the **appellant** being able to show certain reasons for his dissatisfaction). The decisions of a higher court are binding upon lower courts. At the top of the hierarchy is a supreme lawmaking body, but the process of taking an action from a lower court to the highest court may be very time-consuming and costly.

English courts

We can use the English system as an example of how courts relate to one another:

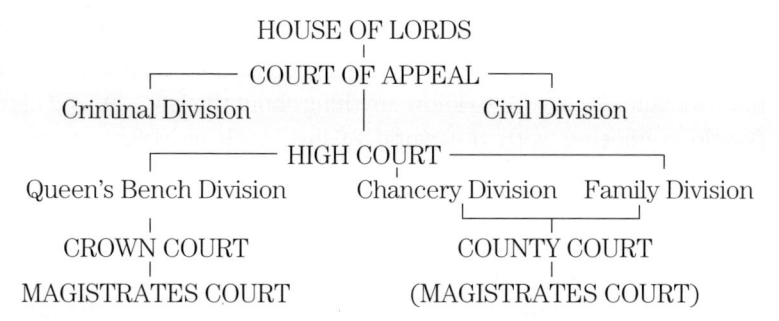

```
                      HOUSE OF LORDS
                            |
            ┌────── COURT OF APPEAL ──────┐
       Criminal Division            Civil Division
                  ┌─────────── HIGH COURT ───────────┐
       Queen's Bench Division   Chancery Division   Family Division
                  |                      └──────┬──────┘
              CROWN COURT                 COUNTY COURT
                  |                             |
          MAGISTRATES COURT            (MAGISTRATES COURT)
```

In general, the division between civil and criminal law is reflected in this system. The Crown Courts, for example, deal exclusively with criminal matters, the County Courts, with civil. However, the Queen's Bench Division of the High Court considers appeals from lower criminal courts, as well as civil matters, and the Magistrates Courts, while mostly concerned with criminal cases, also deal with some civil matters. The highest court, the House of Lords, deals with all matters (including appeals from Scottish and Northern Irish courts).

A criminal case usually begins in a Magistrates Court. Having arrested someone suspected of committing a crime, the police must decide if they have enough evidence to make a formal accusation, or charge. If they charge the suspect, they may release him on the condition that he appear on a certain date at a certain Magistrates Court. This is known as **unconditional bail**. However, the police may instead take the suspect to a magistrate so that he remains in custody until he next appears before a court. The magistrate may decided that it is not necessary to hold the suspect in custody and may agree to unconditional bail, or the magistrate may grant **conditional bail**—that is, release the suspect provided that he puts up some money as security or agrees to surrender his passport or some similar condition. As the lowest criminal court, a Magistrates Court is empowered to hear certain cases only. Some minor cases, such as parking violations, are dealt with only by the magistrates. Some serious crimes, like murder, cannot be heard by the magistrates and must go to the Crown Courts. And there are some offences where the defendant is given the choice of having his case heard in the Magistrates Court or the Crown Court. It takes much longer to have a case heard in the Crown Court, but some defendants prefer it because the facts of the case are decided by a **jury**, that is, ordinary members of the public.

In a Crown Court trial there are twelve jurors. These are ordinary members of the public between the ages of 18 and 70 who are selected at random. They are not paid but are given expenses while they are on **jury service**, which is usually for about two weeks. Service is compulsory, and it cannot normally be avoided without a good reason, such as illness. It is not necessary for a juror to know anything about the law—indeed certain people connected with the world of law, such as solicitors, are not allowed to serve as jurors. This is because the job of the jury is to listen to the case and to decide questions of **fact**. It is the judge's responsibility to guide them on questions of law.

This contrast between law and fact is very important. If a man is on trial for murder, for example, the judge will explain just what the crime of murder means in English law and what the prosecution has to prove. He will explain how the trial will be conducted, summarize the evidence, and tell the jurors what factors they should consider in making their decision. These are questions of law. However, whether the defendant did in fact commit murder or not is a question of fact to be decided by the jurors themselves. It is necessary for at least ten of the twelve to agree.

International comparisons

In some countries such as France (where there are nine jurors), the judges and jurors decide the case together. In the United States juries not only

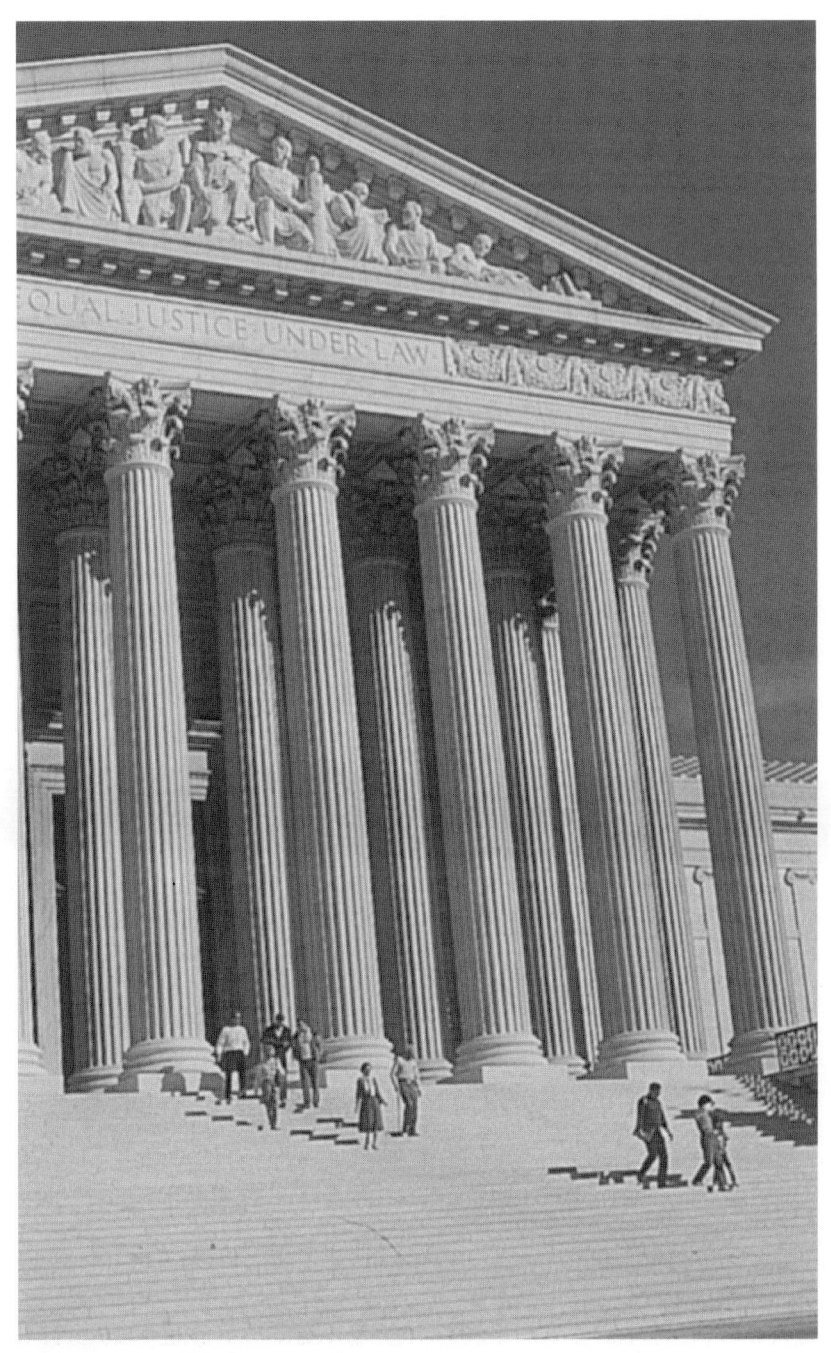

Figure 4.1 *The U.S. Supreme Court.*

decide if the defendant is guilty but sometimes also have a say in what punishment he should receive. Before World War II, Japan also had a jury system, but it was often criticized for the ease with which jurors could be bribed. Now Japan, like South Korea, is a rare example of a modern industrialized country where jurors are not used: all decisions are made by professional judges.

Most countries have special rules for young defendants. Children under ten cannot stand trial at all under English law. Juveniles (those under seventeen) are dealt with in special Magistrates Courts known as Juvenile Courts.

Appeals

A defendant found guilty by the magistrates may appeal against the finding or against the punishment to the local Crown Court, and the Crown Court judge will hear the appeal without a jury. If a defendant has good reason to believe the magistrates have made a mistake about a point of law, then he may appeal to the Queen's Bench Division of the High Court. The appeal system is mostly for the benefit of the defendant, but there are cases of the prosecution successfully appealing for a more severe punishment. In Japan it is even possible for the prosecution to appeal that a not-guilty decision be changed to guilty.

Appeals from the Crown Court go first to the High Court and, in special cases, to the Court of Appeal. Occasionally, a case is carried through this system of appeal all the way to the House of Lords.

The House of Lords is considered the upper house of the British parliament, but its political powers are much more limited than that of the lower house, the House of Commons. Members of the House of Lords are not elected but consist of hereditary peers, peers appointed for life by the government, bishops of the Church of England, and the law lords— peers appointed for life after long service as lawyers. When sitting as a court of appeal it is only the law lords and certain other government-appointed officials who hear cases. Their decisions on both criminal and civil matters bind all other courts. Only the government can overturn a decision of the House of Lords and then, only by passing an Act of Parliament (see Chapter 10).

In many countries, such as Japan and the United States, the highest judicial decisions are made by a Supreme Court. Its members are appointed from the lower courts by the government. Unlike the British House of Lords, Supreme Courts are entirely concerned with legal matters (including the legality of government acts) and have no role in legislation (see Chapter 10).

Lower courts

Apart from the limited civil functions of Magistrates Courts (for example, prevention of family violence), the lowest court in a civil action is a County Court, of which there is one in every town in England and Wales. The judges are always professionals. They may hear matters such as contract and tort disputes, actions regarding claims to land or those regarding the property of a dead person. Cases involving larger amounts of money are heard by one of the divisions of the High Court. The Chancery Division, for example, deals with disputes about trusts, the property of the dead and bankruptcy, among other things. Appeals from the High Court, and most appeals from the County Courts, go to the Court of Appeal.

Some County Courts have authority to grant divorces, but when one of the parties disputes the divorce, it must be transferred to the Family Division of the High Court.

In addition to the courts mentioned above, there are numerous special courts which have been established to make decisions in particular types of dispute. For example, special industrial tribunals deal with disputes over contracts and sexual discrimination in employment matters.

Restrictions

In Britain, as in other nations with democratic systems of government, most court cases are open to the public. This means that any member of the public may witness a court case, although he does not have the right to speak and may be ordered from the court if he tries to interrupt proceedings. But there are some proceedings which are closed. For example, a judge may order that no member of the public be present in a case where a child is giving evidence of sexual abuse which he or she has suffered. The public is also sometimes excluded if the judge feels that a witness or a member of a jury is being threatened by someone watching the proceedings.

There are also restrictions on who may conduct a case in court. In most countries, an ordinary member of the public has the right to present his own case himself. However, although this sometimes happens in lower courts, most people choose to be represented by a professional lawyer, especially in a higher court.

Judicial institutions

Exercises

Comprehension
1 What is the appeal system?
2 What is unconditional bail?
3 Which are questions of law and which are questions of fact?
   a whether an alibi can be believed.
   b whether killing a cat is a crime.
   c whether a guilty defendant should be imprisoned.
4 Name two difference between the American Supreme Court and the British House of Lords.

Discussion
"Legal cases are best decided by professional judges, not by ordinary members of the public."
Write a paragraph containing two points for and two against this statement. Then discuss your answer with other students.

5 Lawyers at work

Professional titles

Although many kinds of people working in or studying legal affairs are referred to as lawyers, the word really describes a person who has become officially qualified to act in certain legal matters because of examinations he has taken and professional experience he has gained. Most countries have different groups of lawyers who each take a particular kind of examination in order to qualify to do particular jobs. In Japan, a lawyer must decide whether he wants to take the examination to become an **attorney**, a **public prosecutor** or a **judge**. In England, the decision is between becoming a **barrister** or a **solicitor**. Barristers specialize in arguing cases in front of a judge and have the right to be heard, **the right of audience**, even in the highest courts. They are not paid directly by clients, but are employed by solicitors. Judges are usually chosen from the most senior barristers, and once appointed they cannot continue to practice as barristers. Solicitors do much of the initial preparation for cases which they then hand to barristers, as well as handling legal work which does not come before a court, such as drawing up wills, and dealing with litigation which is settled out of court. Solicitors also have a right of audience in lower courts, but in higher courts, such as the Court of Appeal, they must have a barrister argue their client's case. In general, it can be said that a barrister spends most of his time either in a courtroom or preparing his arguments for the court and a solicitor spends most of his time in an office giving advice to clients, making investigations and preparing documents. Many people believe the distinction between barristers and solicitors should be eliminated in England, as has already happened in Australia. The government is considering various proposals, but there are arguments for maintaining, as well as removing, the division.

Range of work

Even lawyers with the same qualifications and professional title may be doing very different kinds of work. Most towns in the United States, for example, have small firms of attorneys who are in daily contact with ordinary people, giving advice and acting on matters such as consumer affairs, traffic accident disputes and contracts for the sale of land. Some may also prepare defences for clients accused of crimes. However, in both the United States and other industrialized countries, lawyers are becoming more and more specialized. Working in small firms, lawyers now tend to restrict themselves to certain kinds of work, and lawyers working in large law firms or employed in the law department of a large commercial enterprise work on highly specific areas of law. One lawyer may be employed by a mining company just to prepare contracts for the supply of coal. Another may work for a newspaper advising the editors on libel matters. Another may be part of a Wall Street firm of over a hundred lawyers who specialize in advising stockbrokers on share transactions.

As well as the type of work, the working conditions and pay among members of the legal profession also vary greatly. For some people, the image of a lawyer is someone who leads a very wealthy and comfortable life. However, it should not be forgotten that there are also lawyers whose lives are not so secure. The Wall Street attorney probably earns a high salary, but the small firm giving advice to members of the public on welfare rights or immigration procedures may have to restrict salaries in order to stay in business. There are lawyers in developing countries whose business with fee-paying clients subsidizes the work they agree to do for little or no payment for citizens' rights groups. Lawyers involved in human rights may even find their profession is a dangerous one. Amnesty International research shows that more than 60 lawyers investigating cases against people accused of political crimes were murdered in 1990. In countries where the government ensures that all people have access to a lawyer in an emergency, there are firms that specialize in dealing with people who would not be able to pay for legal services out of their own pocket. For example, in England anyone facing criminal prosecution is entitled to choose a firm of lawyers to represent him. If his income is below a certain level he will not be asked to pay: the firm will keep a record of its costs and will apply to the government-funded Legal Aid Board for payment.

Entering the profession

How does someone become a lawyer? As with doctors and other professionals enjoying a high level of trust because of the specialized knowledge, lawyers are subject to standardized examination and other controls to regulate their competence. In some countries in order to practice as a lawyer it is necessary to get a university degree in law. However, in others, a degree may be insufficient; professional examinations must be passed. In Britain, it is not in fact necessary to have a degree, although nowadays most people entering the profession do. The main requirement is to have pass the Bar Final examination (for barristers) or the Law Society Final examination (for solicitors). Someone with a university degree in a subject other than law needs first to take a preparatory course. Someone without a degree at all may also prepare for the final examination, but this will take several years. In most countries, lawyers will tell you that the time they spent studying for their law finals was one of the worst periods of their life! This is because an enormous number of procedural rules covering a wide area of law must be memorized. In Japan, where there are relatively few lawyers, the examinations are supposed to be particularly hard: less than 5 percent of candidates pass. Even after passing the examination, though, a lawyer is not necessarily qualified. A solicitor in England, for example, must then spend two years as an **articled clerk**, during which time his work is closely supervised by an experienced lawyer, and he must take further courses. A barrister must spend a similar year as a **pupil**.

Regulating the profession

In most countries, once a lawyer is fully qualified he receives a certificate proving his right to sell his services. There are also insurance provisions so that if a lawyer is ever successfully sued by a client for professional incompetence there will be funds available to enable him to pay damages —which may be extremely large in the case of lawyers dealing with property transactions. Even if a lawyer is very competent, he must take care not to break the many rules of procedure and ethics set by the body which regulates his profession. In England, the body regulating the conduct of solicitors is the Law Society. Among other things, it sets rules for lawyers' accounting procedures and investigates complaints against lawyers by their clients. There is also a Solicitor's Disciplinary Tribunal with the power to suspend or even disqualify (or **strike off**) a solicitor. Since its members are themselves solicitors some people fear that it may not be completely impartial. But members of the public do, of course, have the right to sue their solicitor, for example, in an action for negligence (see torts, Chapter 8). However, since the 1967 case of Rondel vs. Worsley and the 1978 case of Saif Ali vs. Sydney Mitchell, barristers in England and Wales may not be sued for negligent services in the courtroom. One reason for this is the fear that almost anyone who lost a court case would try to sue his barrister.

In most legal systems, conversations between a lawyer and his client are **privileged**: the client should know that what he says will not be passed on to someone else without his permission. In theory, this could pose difficult ethical problems for a lawyer; for instance, what should he do in a criminal case if he believes his client is guilty? The lawyer must first decide how sure he is of the client's guilt. It can happen that someone thinks he has committed a crime when in fact he lacked the necessary mental state to be guilty (see Chapter 7). In any case, it is the prosecution's job to prove guilt, not the defence's to prove innocence. A lawyer could therefore defend his client simply by trying to point out weaknesses in the prosecution case.

Another ethical problem for a lawyer arises when he has two clients whose stories contradict each other; for example, each says that he is innocent and the other person is guilty. In such a case the lawyer must transfer one of the clients to another lawyer.

Legalese

Although lawyers come from a variety of backgrounds and do a variety of work, as a profession they often appear rather remote and difficult to understand. Perhaps one reason for this is legalese—the strange and incomprehensible language so many lawyers seem to write and speak. This is not just a feature of English-speaking lawyers. People all over the world complain that they cannot understand court proceedings or legal documents.

Of course all professions have their own jargon. Economists commonly talk about junk bonds (the right to collect a debt which will in fact probably never be repaid); doctors about lacerations (cuts) and contusions (bruises); and English teachers about metalanguage (the words we use to talk about language). The use of some special words can be justified because they refer to matters which are important to a particular profession but not important to most people in everyday life. But sometimes it seems that jargon is a way of creating a mystery about a profession, of distinguishing people on the inside (economist, doctors, teachers) from those on the outside.

In recent times lawyers have made efforts to make their profession less mysterious. After all, their job is supposed to be to clarify matters for the public, not to make them more complicated! This is particularly so in the United States where lawyers openly advertise their services to the public and where special clothes and wigs, still a feature of the English system, have mostly disappeared. But it seems likely that legalese will survive for a long time to come. One reason for this is that old documents and reports of old cases have great importance in law, particularly in common law systems. Another reason is that rewriting laws is a slow and painstaking process. The words must try to cover every eventuality, because people are always looking for a legal loophole, a way of avoiding a legal duty by making use of an ambiguity or an omission in law. Consequently if there is an existing law which has worked for a long time, even a law which contains old language in long and complex sentences, it is easier to retain the old law than write a new one. Even when a government draws up a new law it is often guided by the wording of an older law.

But perhaps the main reason that legalese still survives lies in the nature of law itself. As mentioned in the first chapter, laws are attempts to implement justice, government policy, or just plain common sense. In order to be effective they must be as unambiguous as possible. Everyday language is often very ambiguous, but this does not matter if we are dealing with familiar situations or talking to people we know. The law, however, has to regulate relations between people who neither know nor trust each other and who are in unfamiliar situations. It is an unfortunate necessity that this sometimes requires complex language which has to be explained by experts.

English legalese is characterised by:

1. Words and expressions which have no meaning for non-lawyers, some of them coming from Latin or French. For example:
replevin—the right to take back goods which were illegally removed
nemo dat (quod non habet)—the principle that a person has no right to property acquired from a person who did not legally own it
cy-près—the court's right to grant property to another similar charity if the charity the donor hoped to benefit does not exist
2. Words which look like ordinary English but have a special meaning when used by lawyers. For example:
nuisance—interference with someone's enjoyment of land
consideration—something given or given up on making a contract
3. Formal words which most people understand but which are very old-fashioned. For example:
hereinafter—from now on; below in this document
aforesaid—previously mentioned
4. Very long sentences containing many clauses which limit and define the original statement. The fourth characteristic can perhaps, be best demonstrated by showing an extract from a law in force in England today: the 1837 Wills Act, amended by the 1982 Administration of Justice Act:
"No will shall be valid unless:

(a) it is in writing, and signed by the testator or some other person in his presence and by his direction; and
(b) it appears that the testator intended by his signature to give effect to the will; and
(c) the signature is made or acknowledged by the testator in the presence of two or more witnesses present at the same time; and
(d) each witness either–
(i) attests and signs the will; or
(ii) acknowledges his signature in the presence of the testator (but not necessarily in the presence of any other witness), but no form of attestation shall be necessary."

What exactly does the above mean? If you think it could be written more simply, perhaps you would make a good lawyer!

Exercises

Comprehension
1 Name three differences between barristers and solicitors.
2 What is an articled clerk?
3 Describe two ethical problems a lawyer may face.
4 Give three reasons for the slow pace of modernizing legal language.

Discussion
Ted writes out a will leaving all his property to his wife. He phones his friends Al and Bill to come over and witness the will. While he is waiting for them to arrive he signs his will. When Al and Bill arrive he shows them the will and says "You see I've signed it at the bottom." Al signs his own name and then leaves. While Ted is out of the room saying goodbye to Al, Bill signs the will. When Ted comes back in Bill says, "Look, here's my signature."

Do you think Ted's will would be valid under English law? Discuss this with other students.

Part Two
Legal Principles

6 Contracts

Many people think of a contract as a written agreement between people stating the exact details of promises they have made to each other. For example, when a farm agrees to supply fruit and vegetables to a supermarket, the two businesses will probably draw up a contract containing many clauses about what kind of goods are to be supplied, how often and in what quantities; who is to pay for transport and unpacking; what prices are to be paid, what happens if some of the vegetables arrive in a poor condition and just what is meant by poor condition, and what happens if delivery is made too late for the shop to sell the goods. The contractors will try to think of all the possible circumstances which may arise—even unlikely events such as the vegetables being stolen by a third party while they are being transported.

Different types

However, not all contracts are written. There are many kinds of unwritten agreements between people which the law of most countries describes as contracts. They may continue buying and selling things for years by relying on trust and common sense, and if sometimes there is a disagreement—for example, a supplier fails to deliver goods by the time he said he would—they manage to deal with the problem simply by discussion. However, if the disagreement becomes so serious that they cannot resolve it, they may decide it is necessary to take legal action. One of the most common kinds of legal action is to claim that a contract has existed and that one of them **is in breach of contract** (has broken the agreement). To win such an action it is necessary to show that the agreement can indeed be described as a contract.

There are many everyday transactions which most people never think of as contracts. When you buy a newspaper you simply pick up the paper, pay the price and walk away. But suppose something unusual happens—

perhaps, you discover that the newspaper is not today's but last week's; or there are some pages missing; or the newspaper seller charges you more money than the price written on the newspaper and tells you this is because his transport costs have increased. You may then start to think about what kind of transaction you made in buying the paper and what your rights are. In fact, the simple purchase of a newspaper can indeed be a contract: without writing anything down, maybe without even speaking, you agreed to buy a certain item from a certain person at a certain price.

The problem with unwritten contracts is that it may be very difficult to show evidence of the agreement you made. Can you prove that you bought the newspaper where you did, and not somewhere else? Can you prove how much you paid for it? If the seller claims that you agreed to buy an old newspaper, can you disprove his claim?

Figure 6.1 *Buying and selling in a London market.*

Of course, problems of evidence can arise even when there is a detailed written agreement. Indeed a court of law may decided that the contract consists not just of the written document you possess but includes things that were said but never written down. The contract may even include things that the contractors understood but never talked about. Sometimes an agreement turns out to be a contract even though the persons who made it did not realize this at the time. And sometimes people make agreements which they think are contracts, but when they try to take legal action the court declares that no contract was ever made. (In such a case they may find there is another legal claim they may make, such as an action in tort (see Chapter 8) or in breach of trust (see Chapter 9).

It is therefore important to know just what the law considers a contract to be. In many systems of law there is a written legal code stating exactly what is required to make a contract and what the rights and obligations of contractors are. In case law systems, there is no one code or law defining what a contract is. The law regarding contracts in general is to be found in judgments made by courts and even in legal textbooks. But there are statutes which clarify the law. For example, the Unfair Contract Terms Act, passed in Britain in 1977, specifies circumstances in which a contractor may avoid being obliged by some parts of a contract.

Essential elements

English law textbooks often describe a contract as an agreement which is made between two or more parties and which is binding in law. In order to be binding in law the agreement must include an offer and an acceptance of that offer. The parties must agree to contract on certain terms—that is, they must know what they are agreeing to (but they need not know that their agreement can be described in law as a contract). They must have intended to be legally bound; there would be no contract if, for example, they were just joking when they made the agreement. And **valuable consideration** must have been given by the person to whom a promise was made. In this case, consideration is a legal word to describe something a person has given, or done, or agreed not to do, when making the contract.

When a court is deciding if a contract has been made, it must consider all these elements. In common law countries, the judge will be guided by decisions made in previous cases. If the judge is dealing with a problem which has never arisen before he must make a decision based upon general legal principles, and this decision will become a precedent for other judges in similar cases in the future. The most important principle guiding a judge is whether a reasonable observer of the agreement would decide that it was a contract. But sometimes decisions seem very technical because lawyers try to explain exactly why a decision has been made, even when that decision appears to be obvious common sense. Of course exact explanations are even more important when the decision does not appear to be common sense! By looking at some of the elements of a contract, we can see how important cases have helped to develop English law.

One principle of English contract law mentioned above is that there must be **offer and acceptance**. An advertisement to sell something is not normally considered an offer. If I see an ad in a newspaper offering to sell a car, and I telephone the advertiser and agree to buy it, the seller is not obliged to sell it to me. This is because the law considers that the real offer is when I contact the seller asking to buy the car. The seller may then decide whether to accept or reject my offer. This is the reason a store does not have to sell you goods it displays for sale. (If the seller does accept then one important element of a contract has been made, and if the other elements exist the seller may have an obligation to the buyer.) However, because of the 1893 case of Carlill vs. Carbolic Smoke Ball Company, English law does consider some kinds of advertisements as offers. Carbolic Smoke Ball advertised that they would pay money to anyone who used their medicine and still got the flu. A woman saw the advertisement, bought the medicine, but got the flu, so she asked for the money. The company tried to avoid paying by arguing that their advertisement was not an offer, since it is impossible to make a contract with all the people who might read the advertisement. But the court decided that when Mrs. Carlill saw the ad and bought the medicine she was accepting a specific offer made to her, and so there was a contract and the company was obliged to pay.

Another principle is that the terms being offered and accepted must be certain. However, in the 1932 case of Hillas Company vs. Arcos it was decided that a reference to previous agreements or usual agreements might be certain enough.

Another principle mentioned above is that there is no contract if one of the parties did not intend to be legally bound. This is supported by a case decided in 1605 (Weeks vs. Tybald) when a man joked that he would pay money to any man who would marry his daughter.

What is valuable consideration? The principle behind this phrase is that the law will not enforce an empty promise. For example, if a man offers to wash my car for $10 and I accept, but he goes away and never washes it, I will probably not be able to make him keep his promise unless I have already paid the $10. This is because I have given no consideration: I have not done anything or lost anything because of his offer. However, even if I haven't paid, I may still have given some kind of valuable consideration. For example, perhaps I left the car at home because of his offer to wash it and took a taxi to work. In this case a court might consider that there was an enforceable contract. As a result, I would be able to compel the man either to wash the car or to pay me the taxi fare I had spent. In the 1960 case of Chappel vs. the chocolate manufacturers Nestlé, it was decided that valuable consideration could be of as little value as the used chocolate wrappers which Nestlé asked people to send to them in return for a free record.

Contracts

One very important form of consideration is an agreement not to sue someone. For example, my neighbor makes so much noise that I cannot sleep at night. I have the right to take legal action against her (perhaps in tort, see Chapter 8) but I agree not to do so because she offers to take my mother on vacation to Hawaii. If she then fails to take my mother to Hawaii she is breaking a contract with me and I could choose to take action against her either for breach of contract, or for the original tort. In making my choice I would consider which action would be of most benefit to me.

Most systems of law have similar requirements about offer and acceptance, legal intention, and consideration. They also consider the **capacity** of the contractors; that is, whether they were legally entitled to contract. In English law there are some special rules if one of the contracts is a company, rather that an individual (see Chapter 11), under the age of 18, or insane. Legal systems have rules for interpreting contracts in which one or more contractors made a mistake or was pressured or tricked into making an agreement, and rules for dealing with illegal contracts. For example, under English law a contractor cannot enforce an agreement against another party if the agreement was to commit a crime!

Damages

Once a court decides that there has been a breach of contract, it must then judge how the party in breach must compensate the other party, The usual award is **damages**—monetary compensation. The court must be satisfied that there was a contract, that one party is in breach, and that the other party has suffered some loss because of the breach. In addition to financial loss a plaintiff sometimes tries to claim damages for mental distress caused by the breach of contract. Such claims are less successful in Britain than in the U.S., except for holiday contracts (though often successful in tort actions—see Chapter 8).

A court will award damages only for loss closely connected with the defendant's breach. For example, in the 1949 English case of Victoria Laundry vs. Newman Industries, the defendants were five months late in delivering a new boiler for the laundry. The laundry claimed damages first for profits they would probably have made by being able to increase their regular laundry customers if they had had the boiler on time; and second, for profits they might have made if the the boiler had enabled them to take on new dyeing contracts. The courts decided that the first claim was reasonable, but that the second was too remote. **Remoteness** is an important concept in both contract and tort (see Chapter 8).

In deciding just how much in damages to award, English and American courts try to put the plaintiff into the same financial position that he would have been in if the defendant had carried out the contract properly. For example, in the example mentioned before of a man offering to wash my car and then failing to do so, the court would note that if the contract had been performed I would have a clean car and would not have spent money on a taxi fare. On the other hand I would not have the $10 I agreed to pay the man, nor the value of the gas I would have used in driving my car that day.

Other remedies

Instead of damages, a plaintiff sometimes asks the court to force the other contractor to carry out the contract. In English law this is called **specific performance**. The court will not agree to do this if it causes hardship to the defendant, however, or if it is no longer possible or practical to carry out the contract. Sometimes the court decides to award damages instead of specific performance, and sometimes it awards both. A plaintiff may also ask the court to award an **injunction** against the defendant, that is, to order the defendant not to do something which would be in breach of contract. Specific performance and injunctions are remedies which were developed by the courts of Equity because of inadequacies in the Common Law courts. (see Chapter 2).

Contract law is a central part of legal systems all over the world. It is especially important in international business, where the parties try to specify all the parts of their agreement in a clear written contract so that differences of law and custom between their countries can be avoided. It is sometimes said that some societies are much more "contractual" than others. For example, in the United States people are accustomed to signing written contracts connected with daily life. Some people even draw up a contract with a girlfriend or boyfriend when they start living together in the hope of reducing arguments if they part later. On the other hand, Japanese people rarely even sign contracts of employment when they take a new job, believing that custom and social obligation will be enough to resolve any differences. Perhaps it is not a question of one society being more contractual than another, but rather that in some societies people are more likely to use lawyers and courts to sort out their disagreements, and they therefore feel the need to have precise evidence of their agreements in the form of written contracts.

Contracts

Exercises

Comprehension
1 Which is/are true?
   a Contracts must be written to be legal.
   b A spoken contract is less useful than a written one.
   c Contracts may include matters that were never discussed.
2 Match the word to the description:
   i capacity ii consideration iii damages
   a a disadvantage suffered by someone because of a promise made to him.
   b the legal right to make a contract.
   c a court order to carry out a contract.
   d compensation for breach of contract.
3 Explain "remoteness."
4 Name and explain three remedies a common law court may make to the victim of a breach of contract.

Discussion
Mr. A invites Ms. B out to dinner and reserves a table at an expensive restaurant in the countryside. He rents a car to take her to the restaurant, but when he arrives at her house he finds she is out. After waiting an hour he gives up and goes to the movies. He later discovers Ms. B had changed her mind when another boyfriend invited her out.

Consider whether, under English law, Mr. A or Ms. B might be in breach of any contracts, and what compensation might be demanded. Discuss this with other students.

7 Criminal Law

What is a crime?

In Chapter 3, crime was categorized as a part of public law—the law regulating the relations between citizens and the state. Crimes can be thought of as acts which the state considers to be wrong and which can be punished by the state. There are some acts which are crimes in one country but not in another. For example, it is a crime to drink alcohol in Saudi Arabia, but not in Egypt. It is a crime to smoke marijuana in England, but not (in prescribed places) in the Netherlands. It is a crime to have more than one wife at the same time in France, but not in Indonesia. It is a crime to have an abortion in Ireland, but not in Spain. It is a crime not to flush a public toilet after use in Singapore, but not in Malaysia. In general, however, there is quite a lot of agreement among states as to which acts are criminal. A visitor to a foreign country can be sure that stealing, physically attacking someone or damaging their property will be unlawful. But the way of dealing with people suspected of crime may be different from his own country.

Figure 7.1 *An arrest during a student demonstration.*

Elements of proof

In many legal systems it is an important principle that a person cannot be considered guilty of a crime until the state proves he committed it. The suspect himself need not prove anything, although he will of course help himself if he can show evidence of his innocence. The state must prove his guilt according to high standards, and for each crime there are precise elements which must be proven. In codified systems, these elements are usually recorded in statutes. In common law systems, the elements of some crimes are detailed in statutes; others, known as "common law crimes," are still described mostly in case law. Even where there is a precise statute, the case law interpreting the statute may be very important since the circumstances of each crime may be very different.

For example, the crime of **theft** is defined in England under the 1968 Theft Act as:
> dishonestly appropriating property belonging to another with the intention of permanently depriving the other of it.

There are further definitions of each element of the definition, such as appropriating, which may mean taking away, destroying, treating as your own, and selling. The same Act also defines in detail crimes such as **burglary** (entering someone's land without permission intending to steal or commit an act of violence) and **robbery** (using force or threats in order to steal from someone). Although the Theft Act was intended to cover many possible circumstances, it is still often necessary for the courts to refer to case law in order to apply the Act to a new case. For example, in the 1985 case of R. vs. Brown, the defendant argued he couldn't be guilty of burglary since he reached through the window of a house without actually going inside. However, the court decided a person can be judged to have "entered" a building if gets close enough to be able to remove something from it.

There are usually two important elements to a crime: (i) the criminal act itself; and (ii) the criminal state of mind of the person when he committed the act. In Anglo-American law these are known by the Latin terms of (i) **Actus Reus** and (ii) **Mens Rea**. The differences between these can be explained by using the crime of murder as an example.

In English law there is a rather long common law definition of **murder**: The unlawful killing of a human being under the Queen's Peace, with malice aforethought, so that the victim dies within a year and a day.

Malice aforethought refers to the mens rea of the crime and is a way of saying that the murderer intended to commit a crime. Of course, the court can never know exactly what was in the head of the killer at the time of the killing, so it has the difficult task of deciding what his intentions must have been. The judgments in many recent cases show that English law is constantly developing its definition of intent.

There is a different definition of mens rea for each crime. Sometimes the defendant must have intended to do a particular thing. In murder, however, it is interesting that the defendant need not have intended to kill, but just to have wounded someone seriously. He need not even have had a direct intention; in some cases, a defendant has been found guilty if he killed someone because of recklessness—not caring about the dangers. Several recent cases have considered the problem of whether recklessness means acting even though you know there is a high risk of danger or acting without thinking about risks which a reasonable person ought to consider. In other crimes, it is enough to have been negligent or careless without any clear intention or even recklessness.

The rest of the murder definition refers to the actus reus. The prosecution must show that the suspect did in fact cause the death of someone. It must be an unlawful killing under the "Queen's Peace" because there are some kinds of killing which the state considers lawful—for example, when a soldier kills an enemy soldier in a time of war. A time limit is specified in order to avoid the difficulties of proving a connection between an act and a death that takes place much later. This may be especially relevant in the case of a victim who has been kept alive for many months on a hospital life support machine.

In deciding if the defendant's act caused death, the court must be sure that the act was a **substantial cause** of the result. In the 1983 case of Pagett, the defendant held a girl in front of him to prevent police from firing at him. But he himself shot at a policeman and one of the policeman fired back, accidentally killing the girl. The court decided that the defendant could have foreseen such a result when he shot at the policeman from behind the girl, and, as a result, his act was a substantial cause of the death. In the 1959 case of Jordon, the defendant stabbed a man who was then taken to a hospital where he started to recover. But the man died when hospital staff gave him drugs to which he was allergic. In this case the court decided that the hospital's error was the substantial cause of death rather than the attack by the defendant.

In some cases doing nothing at all may be considered an actus reus, such as in the 1918 case of R. vs. Gibbons and Proctor, in which a child starved to death because his father did not feed him.

In general, if the prosecution fails to prove either actus or mens, the court must decide there was no crime and the case is over. However, there are a small number of crimes for which no mens rea need be proved. For example, in Alphacell vs. Woodward (1972), waste from a factory entered a river because of a blocked pipe. The factory owners were able to show that they had no intention to pollute, were not reckless, and were not even negligent since they had carried out all the checks required. Nevertheless a court found them guilty under the 1951 Rivers (Prevention of Pollution) Act. The court decided that the Act was intended to encourage very high standards and so it was enough simply for the prosecution to show that pollution from the factory had entered the river.

Defenses

If actus and mens have been proved, a defendant may still avoid guilt if he can show he has a **defense**—a reason the court should excuse his act. Different systems of law recognize different and usually limited sets of defenses. For example, English law sometimes allow the defense of **duress**—being forced to commit a crime because of threats that you or someone else will be harmed if you don't. Duress may be used as a defense against the charge of murder as a secondary party (helping the murderer), but is not available if the defendant is charged as the principal murderer.

Another defense is that of **insanity**. In most countries a person cannot be found guilty of a crime if in a doctor's opinion he cannot have been responsible for his actions because of mental illness. But this defense requires careful proof. If it is proven the defendant will not be sent to a prison, but instead to a mental hospital.

It might be argued that a person is not responsible for his actions if he is **intoxicated**—drunk or under the influence of drugs. In fact, an intoxicated person may not even know what he is doing and thus lacks mens rea. However, in Britain and many other countries, there is a general principle that people who knowingly get themselves intoxicated must be held responsible for their acts. Consequently, intoxication is not a defense.

Nearly every system of law recognizes the defense of **self-defense**. In English law, a defendant can avoid guilt for injuring someone if he can convince the court that the force he used was reasonable to protect himself in the circumstances. In some countries, shooting an unarmed burglar would be recognized as self-defense, but in other it might be considered unreasonable force.

The concept of defense should not be confused with that of **mitigation**—reasons your punishment should not be harsh (see Chapter 19). If a person has a defense, the court finds him not guilty. It is only after being found guilty that a defendant may try to mitigate his crimes by explaining the specific circumstances at the time of the crime. In France, the defense of

crime of passion is sometimes used to lessen the sentence: that your act was directly caused by the unreasonable behavior of your lover.

Although most criminal laws in the world refer to acts of violence or theft, there are laws regulating almost every kind of human behavior: for example, what we do with our land (Chapter 10); what we say and write (Chapters 15, 16); how we run our businesses (Chapter 11); even what we wear. Sometimes governments "create new crimes" by identifying a form of behavior and passing a new law to deal with it. In most industrialized countries existing theft laws were not adequate to deal with computer crimes where complex kinds of information are stolen, altered or used to deceive other, and, thus, new laws have been passed.

Technical change is one reason criminal law is one of the fastest growing areas of the law. Another reason is that the number of crimes committed in some countries seem to be increasing rapidly—although sometimes it is not clear whether people are breaking the law more, being caught more, or reporting other people's crimes more. One more reason is that different societies—or perhaps it is different governments—continually review their ideas of what should and shouldn't be a considered crime. Homosexual acts, suicide and blasphemy (attacking religion, see Chapter 16) were once crimes in all European countries, but have now mostly been decriminalized. On the other hand, discrimination against someone on the grounds of race or sex was not acknowledged as a crime until relatively recently, and is still not recognized in some countries (Chapter 18). Recent cases of **euthanasia** (shortening the life of a sick person) are causing re-evaluations of the concept of murder.

Criminal law

Exercises

Comprehension

1 What are the two important elements of a crime which the prosecution must prove?
2 Which is/are true? In England, a person may be guilty of murder if he killed someone
   a intentionally.
   b having intended only to injure him or her slightly.
   c without caring about the dangers of his actions.
3 What is the difference between a defence and mitigation?
4 Name and explain three defences.

Discussion

"Criminals need help more than punishment."

Write a paragraph containing two arguments for and two against this statement. Then discuss your answer with other students.

8   Torts

Many wrongs in society are neither punished as crimes nor remedied as breaches of contract. Suppose a workman accidentally drops a brick on my head when I am walking past a construction site, or suppose a neighbor's bonfire gets out of control and damages my house. In either case, there is no contract between me and the other party and it is unlikely anyone will be prosecuted for a crime unless intention or recklessness can be shown. In order to get compensation for such injury or damage, my best course will probably be an action in the law of torts.

The concept of **tort**—a wrongful act among private individuals—exists in most modern systems of law. The word itself means "wrongful" in French, but is used in the mostly English-speaking common law traditions.

Comparison with crimes

The definitions of many torts closely resemble definitions of crimes. For example, the tort of **conversion** in English law covers taking, destroying or selling someone else's goods, as does the crime of theft. When a tort is committed, the same act is often also a crime. But the essential difference between torts and crimes is that the former are the subject of civil law disputes between private individuals, and the latter are prosecuted by the state (see Chapter 3). Sometimes an individual takes an action in the law of tort because he has been the victim of the crime but has gained no benefit from the criminal prosecution. Sometimes there is no criminal prosecution because the police do not feel they have enough evidence or they feel that the matter is more of a private dispute than one involving public law and order. And sometimes it is difficult to find a criminal law which covers a tortious act. For example, simply entering land without the owners's permission is not a crime in English law. It is, however, the tort of **trespass**. The police cannot take any action unless the trespasser commits certain crimes such as displacing the legal occupier and refusing to leave, threatening violence, or damaging property. In order to prevent trespass or to get compensation for any inconvenience caused, the occupier will therefore have to start a civil action in tort.

There are other differences between torts and crimes. As for all civil actions, the standard of proof required is lower than in criminal prosecutions. And for many torts it is not necessary to show any particular mental element, so tort actions are often appropriate in the case of accidents.

Comparison with broken contracts

There are also important differences between the law of tort and the law of contract. For example, even if a person suffers directly from someone else's breach of contract, he does not have the capacity to sue in contract unless he was a party to the contract (there are a few special exceptions). But he may be able to show that the breach represents a tort committed against him. In general, almost anyone may sue or be sued in tort—a child, someone who is mentally sick, even someone who has died. In such cases, the action will be conducted in or against their name by another authorized person. However, in some torts there are specific rules about who may sue or be sued. The occupier of an apartment, for example, may sue in the tort of **nuisance** if he is injured by broken glass falling from his neighbor's apartment. But if a visitor is also injured he has no right under this tort and would have to seek another action, such as in the tort of **negligence** (breach of a legal duty of care—see below).

Under the concept of **vicarious liability** (liability on behalf of someone else) it may be possible to sue the employer of a person who commits a tort in the normal course of his employment. This may be useful if high damages are being sought, since a defendant cannot be forced to pay more money than he has.

Of course not every wrong committed in society is remediable in tort; the plaintiff has to show that he has suffered an action recognized as a tortious one, and he must show that his relation to the **tortfeaser** (committer of the tort) gives him the legal capacity to sue. Nevertheless, the law of tort covers a wide area of wrongdoings which may help those not in a contractual relationship. The tort of nuisance covers many situations where even though no property is taken or trespassed upon, your enjoyment of land is interfered with, for example, by a neighbor who creates too much noise or whose rubbish causes unpleasant smells. The tort of **defamation** covers attacks against someone's reputation through the written or spoken word. The tort of negligence has particularly wide application. Some torts are known as **statutory torts**—the kind of breach of duty which must be proved is defined in a statute. For example, injury suffered because of defective factory equipment may lead to a negligence action regulated by the 1969 Employers Liability Act.

It often happens that a person who suffers a wrong finds that he has the choice in the law of contract to sue either in the law of contract or in tort. For example, if I am injured in a taxi because of the driver's careless driving, I could sue the driver for breach of an unwritten contract to take me to the

Figure 8.1 *A possible nuisance?*

airport, or I could sue him for the tort of negligence. The choice may depend upon which case is easier to prove and whether I am likely to get larger damages under the law of contract or the law of tort.

In contract, the aim of damages is to put the plaintiff in the position that he would have been in if the contract had been performed; damages in tort are to restore the position there would have been if the tort had not occurred. Sometimes these two positions are different and represent different amounts of monetary compensation.

As in contract, if the harm suffered is considered too remote from the defendant's actions, damages are not payable. However, the rules regarding remoteness in tort are different from those in contract, coming from different cases. In the 1921 case Re Polemis, a dockworker dropped some wood into the hold of a ship; it caused a spark which led to a fire because some gas had leaked into the hold. Although the dockworker could not have know about the gas the fire was considered a direct consequence of his mistake and legal action could be taken against him or his employers. However, the 1961 Wagon Mound case established the principle that a defendant is only liable for consequences that were reasonably foreseeable. In this case the defendant company was not liable for a fire which resulted from oil leading from their ship, floating across water and being ignited by a spark.

Requirements of proof

The requirements of proof differ for each tort. Sometimes it is necessary to show a degree of carelessness, as in the tort of negligence. In others, a defendant may be liable even if he was not at fault, such as the **strict liability** (see Chapter 7) tort where an animal you keep on your land manages to escape and cause damage. In some torts it is necessary for the plaintiff to show that he has suffered actual damage or injury, such as the tort of nuisance, whereas in others no harm need be shown. For example, in the tort of **false imprisonment**, it is enough to show that you have been detained against your will, even if it was for a short time, no force or threats were used, and you were not harmed or inconvenienced. However, since damages are related to the harm suffered, it is not likely someone would sue in such a case unless he was seeking another kind of remedy, such as injunction (see Chapter 6).

Although some torts refer to specific kinds of wrongdoing, the tort of negligence is used in many different situations: when someone falls into a hole in the road, for example, or is given the wrong treatment by a hospital, or is injured by faulty machinery at work. The number of negligence actions is increasing all over the world, as is the amount of damages. In the United States, doctors, dentists and lawyers are often sued for millions of dollars. This has in turn increased the cost of many services since such professionals have to pay very high insurance premiums to cover themselves in case they are ever successfully sued.

To win an action in negligence, a plaintiff must show that a **duty of care** existed between himself and the defendant at the time of the tort; that this duty of care has been breached; and that damage or injury has been suffered because of this.

Some duties of care have been long recognized by the law and do not require much proof, for example, the duty of a doctor to exercise a high degree of care in treating his patient. But other duties depend upon the situation and must be proven. For example, what duty does a passerby owe to the victim of a road accident when he tries to give emergency aid? In English law a general principle has been developed that we owe a duty to people closely affected by our actions to avoid causing harm which we could reasonably have foreseen.

Using this principle, a large body of case law has been created to clarify the duty of care in different areas of life. In developing case law, the courts have also been guided by common sense and public policy. One aim is to allow people to get just compensation for harm suffered without letting them forget their own responsibility to take care of themselves. Another is to discourage a big increase in the number of civil actions because of the amount of time the courts would need to deal with this.

Nevertheless the number and variety of negligence actions increases year by year. At one time cases were only actionable if personal injury or damage to property could be shown, but it is now possible to claim for financial loss connected to this. Indeed, a person may sue for economic loss alone if this resulted from a negligent false statement, as in the case of a garage owner whose business failed to make profits because the previous owner had not told him a new road being built would divert cars away from the garage (Esso Petroleum, 1976). Damages are now awarded for the mental distress caused by an accident, as well as the physical suffering. And it may even be possible for a third party to sue after suffering nervous shock as the result of witnessing an accident.

Exercises

Comprehension
1 Give two reasons torts are often easier to prove than crimes.
2 Which is/are true? "Vicarious liability" means
   a legal responsibility for the actions of another.
   b the possibility of suing a company instead of suing an individual employee.
   c a way of getting higher damages.
3 Name and briefly describe five torts mentioned in this chapter.
4 Explain "duty of care."

Discussion
"Instead of suing the city authorities, people who fall into holes in the street should accept responsibility for their own carelessness."

Write a paragraph containing two arguments for and two against this statement. Then discuss your answer with other students.

9 Trusts

A **trust** is an agreement whereby property is held and controlled by someone on behalf of someone else. A common example of this is where someone dies and leaves money for grandchildren who are too young to deal with it themselves. The money will be held in the name of **trustees**—for example, the children's parents. They will be the legal owners of the money and will have the power to invest and make other decisions about it. But they are required to act only in the interests of the children, known as the **beneficiaries** of the trust, and they must not make any personal profit.

The concept of a trust is a creation of the law of equity (see Chapter 2). It is thus unique to common law countries such as the United States and most of the Commonwealth, although many countries, such as Japan have statutes which effectively impose trusts in certain cases. Even though the common law and equitable systems have long been merged, we still talk about the beneficiaries of a trust having an "equitable" interest in the property, the trustees a "legal" interest. In addition, the original intention of equity still survives: to limit the powers of those who have legal rights but owe special responsibilities to others.

Different types

Some trusts are known as **express trusts**, having been intentionally created by someone with property to transfer (a **settlor**). The example in the opening paragraph is an express private trust. Other trusts are **implied**—the law presumes that the settlor intended to create a trust even though he did not expressly say so. In all of these cases, the person appointed to be trustee has a choice whether or not to accept the appointment when the trust is created. But some trusts are **constructive**: the law imposes a trust and obliges the legal owner of property to consider the beneficial interest of another person. A common example of this is when the seller of a house is obliged to give a proportion of the proceeds to a former spouse who once lived there with him. Directors of companies and solicitors are often in the position of a constructive trustee regarding property under their control.

Enforcers and administrators

Unlike contracts, trusts can be enforced by a third party, the beneficiary. In addition, it is not necessary for the beneficiary to have given any consideration (see Chapter 6). If the trustee fails to do his duty he may be liable in an action for breach of trust. This may result in an injunction, or even a personal action against him, for example, to gain property which has been misappropriated.

A trust may have a single trustee or several. It may also have several beneficiaries. Sometimes trustees are also beneficiaries under the trust. A trust may also be administered by a trust corporation, as in the case of public charities (see below).

Trust law is also relevant to the administration of property when someone dies. Under Anglo-American law the dead person's property passes immediately to administrators (called **executors** if the dead person left a will). Administrators and executors are not technically trustees since their powers and duties are defined in statute (for example, the Administration of Estates Act in England). However, since they become the legal owners of the dead person's property, and hold it on trust until they have paid debts and taxes and can pass it on to those entitled to inherit, their position is very similar to that of a trustee.

Requirements

When creating an express private trust, the settlor creates rights and obligations that may survive his death. Certain conditions must therefore be met if the trust is to be valid in law. In English law, for example, there must be certainty that a trust is being created, what the trust property is, and who the beneficiaries are. When a husband left property to his widow to use "in any way she thinks best for the benefit of herself and her family," it was held that there was no certainty he had intended to create a trust, and so she was free to use the property as she wanted (Lambe vs. Eames, 1871). On the other hand, when a Mr. Constance opened a bank account in his own name but made arrangements for his lover to draw money from it, this was certain enough evidence of her rights as a beneficiary (Paul vs. Constance, 1977). When someone's will declared a trust over "the bulk (greater part) of my estate," it was held there could be no trust since no one could say how much property should be in the trust (Palmer vs. Simonds, 1854). A trust for the benefit of a firm's employees, former employees, and their relatives was held to be certain enough even though the number of beneficiaries might be very large (Re. Baden, 1973). One of the judges in this case suggested that a trust for the benefit of "the residents of London," would not be valid, however; although it is certain who the beneficiaries are to be, the number would be so great the trust could not be administered.

When creating an express public (charitable) trust, it is not necessary to be so certain about the beneficiaries. It is enough if the person giving the property (the **donor**) has shown a clear intention to benefit charity. In many countries charities can claim tax exemptions and so governments have clear rules about what may be considered a charity. In Japan, for example, over two hundred thousand new religious groups are registered as exempt from income tax having satisfied certain requirements under the civil code, such as the practice of "religious activities and possession of specific beliefs." In English law, in order to be considered a charity, an organization must work for one of four purposes: the relief of poverty, the advancement of religion, the advancement of education, or the benefit of the community. The last category is very vague. Trusts for the welfare of animals, for orphans, and for the fire brigade, have been allowed under this category, but a trust to look after a specific animal would not be allowed. Amnesty International was disallowed because it was held to have a political element. And an organization opposed to experiments on animals was disallowed because it was held that on balance such experiments were to the benefit of the community.

Trusts

Exercises

Comprehension

1 What is the difference between an express trust and an implied trust?
2 Name three differences between a trust and a contract.
3 Which is/are true? To be valid in English law a trust must
   a be in operation before the settlor dies.
   b make clear what the trust property is.
   c be for charitable purposes.
4 Why do you think English law permits trusts for the welfare of animals in general but not for one animal in particular? Discuss this with another student.
5 Give examples of three situations in which trusts occur.

Discussion

"Religious groups should not be exempt from tax." Write a paragraph containing two arguments for and two against this statement. Then discuss your answer with other students.

10 Land law

In most legal systems a distinction is made between land and other kinds of property. Sometimes land is called real estate in contrast to personal estate or immovable assets in contrast to movable assets such as furniture and vehicles. In this chapter "land" refers not only to a piece of ground, but to any buildings upon it.

All over the world people think of land as the most important form of property. A subsistence farmer in a developing country needs a secure right to use a piece of land in order to grow food for his family. A city dweller needs shelter from cold and heat and theft. Many people spend all their working lives paying instalments on a house or apartment so that they will own the place in which they live when they stop work and will have something of value to pass on to their children.

Of course, it is business property—shops, factories, offices, hotels—that is the most valuable land of all. In 1993, just one square meter of commercial land in Hong Kong was valued at around US$20. Land is not just a site for dwellings or workplaces, but a commodity which can be sold, rented out or used as security in order to borrow money which can be used to buy shares or to buy other pieces of land.

Complexity

It is not surprising that the law regulating such a valuable form of property tends to be very complex and have a long history. When transferring land both the old and new owners want to be very clear about exactly what has been transferred. Is the house you want to spend all your savings on in a good condition? Do you have the right to use the small piece of ground at the back of the house? If the fence between your house and the next one falls down, who is responsible for it? Are there plans to build a new road right next door, and did the seller know about these plans? Can you even be sure that the seller is the true owner of the land and entitled to sell it to you? A person renting land (a **tenant**) will also want to know exactly what his rights and responsibilities are, especially if he is planning to live on that land for a long time or wants to be able to sell the right to rent the land to another person. How long can he use the property? Can the owner increase the rent or make him leave? Who must pay for repairs—the owner or the tenant?

As well as being complex, some systems of land law are rather old and include procedures and language which seem mysterious to non-lawyers.

Land law

Figure 10.1 *The most expensive land on earth.*

In part, this is because governments are often reluctant to change the laws relating to land: changes require detailed revisions of detailed laws, and landowners may be alarmed by new rules relating to their most precious possession. Having had less political change than most countries, England still uses many land laws which originated hundreds of years ago. Some landowners can produce written records which show how their land has passed through dozens of owners over the years through gifts or sales (although to prove **title**—that he is the legal owner of the land—the landholder only has to show that he or previous owners held the land legally for a certain number of years.) Even in France and the United States, where political revolutions led to the re-writing of the legal system, some people can show a right to land which originated in a family ancestor long before the revolution.

Estate in English law

In 1925, several laws were passed in England in an attempt to simplify the system of holding and transferring land. These laws recognised two **estates** in land. An estate is a right to possess land for a defined period of time, and the two estates recognised are (i) "fee simple absolute in possession" and (ii) "term of years absolute." The first means that the landholder owns the land throughout his life unless he sells or gives it to someone else. Eventually, this land will pass to his **heirs** (people entitled to the property of someone after he dies: see previous chapter). The second is a right to hold land for a certain fixed period, after which the land returns to the holder of the estate "absolute in possession."

We often call the first estate a **freehold** and the second a **leasehold**, or **lease**. All land is ultimately held by a freeholder, but sometimes it is the freeholder who is using the land, and sometimes it is a leaseholder. In England a majority of people living in houses own the freehold, but people living in apartments usually own a lease. When they buy an apartment they will want to buy as long a lease as possible from the freeholder—for example, 99 years. Often the leaseholder (or **lessee**) has the right to sell his lease to someone else, but of course he can only sell the right to use the land for the number of years remaining on the lease. Until the lease ends, he has the right to possess the land exclusively: even the freeholder has no right to enter the land without the leaseholder's permission. However, the contract he signed with the freeholder will require him to fulfil certain obligations, such as paying rent (ground rent) and keeping buildings in a good condition. The obligations, or **covenants**, which the leaseholder and freeholder owe to each other can be very complicated. For example, they must decide who is to pay if expensive repairs need to be done. Even a 99 year lease could be ended (**forfeited**) if the lessee breaks an important agreement such as rent payment.

It seems likely that the leasehold system for owning an apartment will be changed in the near future. In other countries which inherited the English system of law, apartment owners usually hold a **commonhold**—a share in the freehold of the land on which the whole apartment building stands. This system is similar to the way apartments are owned in continental-law countries and enables an owner to sell his apartment without the worry that his lease is too short.

Legal interests

As well as these two estates, or ways of holding your land, English law since 1925 has recognized four legal interests over land held by someone else. The first is an **easement**, such as a neighbor's right to use a footpath over your land, or your right not to have buildings or trees on your land block light to his windows. The second is a **rent–charge**—someone's right to charge a landholder a periodical sum of money. The third is a **legal mortgage**—an interest in property given as a form of security to someone who has lent the landholder money. If the money is repaid the interest ends. However, if the landholder fails to pay his debt by a certain time, the money-lender, or **mortgagee**, may have the right to take the property from the borrower, or **mortgagor**. Mortgages are very important in land law because when most people buy an initial house or apartment they have to borrow a lot of money from a mortgagee such as a bank or a building society. The last legal interest is a **right of entry**. The right of a freeholder to enter a lessee's property if he fails to pay rent is an example of a right of entry.

Land transfer

Someone who buys land needs to know exactly what rights and obligations are attached to the land. Although it is possible to deal directly with the seller, most people employ a solicitor to handle the complicated business of land transfer, known as **conveyancing**. In fact, even after the simplifications of 1925, which reduced the system to two kinds of legal estate and four kinds of legal interest, there still exist many kinds of "equitable" interest (see previous chapter) which the buyer and seller need to know about. For example, even if the freehold you want to buy is registered in the name of only one person, you should make sure the spouse of the freeholder does not have the right to continue living in the property after it has been sold!

When investigating the rights attached to land, solicitors used to examine **title deeds**—documents recording transfers of the property over many years. In Britain there is now a land registry which makes investigation of title easier because it is a central register describing the land, the landholder, and third party rights. However, not all land in Britain has yet been recorded on the register, and there are some land rights which need not be recorded there. Even if land has been registered, the solicitor still has many things to check, such as possible plans of the local council to build noisy roads near the house. Any mistakes he makes could cost the buyer a lot of money. Conveyancing is one of the areas in which solicitors sometimes get sued by clients.

Short-term possession

Another important area of land law concerns types of possession for shorter and less secure terms than freeholds and leases—for example, where a person living in property pays money to a **landlord** every week in return for permission to live there. The landlord is usually the freeholder or the leaseholder of the property, but sometimes he himself is paying rent to someone else. Sometimes it is not easy to decide whether a tenancy is a lease or only a **license**. Generally, a licensee does not have as much security as a lessee. For example, if he fails to pay the rent, his landlord may be able to repossess the property more easily and more quickly than a freeholder can get his land back from a leaseholder. However, many legal systems have laws to protect such land-users. In Britain, for example, the Landlord and Tenant Act requires landlords to give certain periods of warning to tenants if they want to repossess their property, and it provides means for tenants to negotiate a reasonable period of time in which to pay rent **arrears** (over due rent). Under the 1988 Housing Act, there are Rent Tribunals which sometimes have the power to reduce rents which they consider too high. There are also special laws concerning tenants who rent land in order to run a business. Usually, however, there is greater protection for someone who rents land to live on.

Regulation of private and public land

As well as laws to regulate relations between tenants and landlords of land, or between purchasers and vendors, there is a large amount of

Land law

law regulating our usage of the land we own or occupy. There is an old saying: "An Englishman's home is his castle"—no matter how many laws control our life in society, we are free to live on and use our private land as we wish. But in England, as in every country in the world, such freedom is limited. If we make too much noise, or pollute our neighbor's air, we may face an action in the tort of nuisance (mentioned in Chapter 8). If we want to build something or extend an existing building, we may need planning permission from the local authority. Indeed, there are cases of a local council forcing someone to pull down a new building or extension because it did not comply with regulations about size, height, design or building materials. When buying a house, the purchaser needs to be especially careful that there are no new constructions which were built without permission.

Most countries have regulations about using land for business purposes. In England, for example, a private house cannot be turned into a store without permission, and the local authorities will only give permission if they think the community needs such a store and that this business will not disturb the neighbors. In Japan, each local area is divided into zones, some just for residential housing, some just for industry, some allowing certain kinds of businesses, schools, or light industry.

There is also a large area of law concerned with publically owned land—for example, highways, pavements, parks. The owner of such land may be the state or a local government authority. In many cases, the land laws appropriate to individuals are also appropriate in dealings involving public land; however, in addition, there is a large body of national legislation, and local legislation (in England called **bylaws**) to regulate the use of such land. For example, a town council may own land that it sets aside as a place for parking. There will be bylaws about how long you can park there and how much it costs. Many governments designate certain areas of natural beauty as national parks. Sometimes the land is owned by the state and sometimes it continues to be privately owned, but the occupants have to obey strict rules about their use of the land. Many old houses, parks, footpaths and coastal areas in Britain are owned by the National Trust and National Trust for Scotland—large, charitable organizations (see previous chapter).

Exercises

Comprehension
1 Why is land law often old and complex?
2 Which is/are true?
   a The same piece of land can have both a freeholder and a leaseholder at the same time.
   b Most English apartment dwellers own a lease rather than a freehold.
   c A leaseholder cannot sell his lease to anyone except the freeholder.
3 In what situation may a bank take possession of someone's house?
4 Name two laws in Britain that help to protect tenants.
5 What is planning permission?

Discussion
"Landlords should have as much freedom in setting rents as shopkeepers have in setting prices."
Write a paragraph containing two arguments for and two against this statement. Then discuss your answer with other students.

Part Three
The Law in Practice

11   Running a business

Every year there is an increase in the number of laws, lawyers, and legal cases in the courts. To a large extent, this increase is due to the economic growth in the world; more business means more transactions, more possibilities for conflict and confusion, and, consequently more legal activity to regulate business. If you set up a business, even a very small one, you will buying and selling products and services, and perhaps, employing people, buying or renting land, and borrowing money. In order to engage in all of these activities, you need to have some knowledge of basic legal principles such as contract, tort, and land law. And you will need to know about any laws specifically relevant to your kind of business, such as statutes regulating companies. If you do not run your business honestly you may also need a knowledge of criminal law! In 1991, a series of Japanese companies faced fines or suspension of activities for making illegal payments to certain clients. Imelda Marcos has been charged both in Manila and in the United States with improperly handling millions of dollars while her husband was President of the Philippines.

Nearly every general area of the law is relevant to running a business, and nearly every country has its own set of laws designed specifically to regulate business. The attempts of the European Community to create a single market by 1993 show just how difficult it can be to harmonize business laws. In this chapter we will try to make some sense of this complex area of the law by taking English law as a model and making some international comparisons. Throughout the world, most businesses face similar problems; they must determine their organizational form; duties to clients; investors and employees; tax liabilities; and ability to minimize losses if the business fails.

Unlike many legal systems, English law has never developed a comprehensive code of company law. Instead, the relevant law is found partly in cases decided according to the principles of common law and equity and partly in statutes. Between 1985 and 1986, a series of statutes was passed to consolidate many previous statutes. The most important of these was the 1985 Companies Act.

Organization

If you want to set up a business under English law, the first question to consider is whether or not to form a **limited company** (or **corporation**). A corporation is a kind of artificial legal person, with the right to sue and be sued. It may consist of a single person, or several persons, but in each case it has a legal identity separate from these individuals. The members of a limited company have **limited liability**. This means that if the business has difficulties, the members can be made to pay its debts only up to a certain limit. Normally this limit is the amount unpaid on shares they hold (**limited by shares**), or the amount they have guaranteed to contribute to company assets (**limited by guarantee**). The company's liability itself is not limited; as long as the business has money or assets, creditors may sue. But they cannot sue the members as individuals beyond their stated limits. In Britain, a limited liability company has the word "limited" or the abbreviation "ltd." after its names. The equivalent to this kind of company can be found all over the world: for example Société Accréditée (SA) in France and Kabushiki Gaisha in Japan.

Certain very large companies are registered as public limited companies (PLC) They raise capital by selling shares to the general public, and these shares are listed on the Stock Exchange.

Selling shares is one of the ways in which companies raise capital. A share is ownership of a proportion of the company, and thus the right to a proportion of any profit it makes (**dividend**). Shareholders cannot insist on the payment of a dividend every year, since this is up to the directors to decide. But if they are dissatisfied with the management of the company, as members they have the right to remove the directors (see below). The more shares a member holds, the more voting rights he will have in general meetings. Shares may be acquired when the company is first set up; or at a later share issue. Or they may be bought or received from an existing shareholder. Sometimes a company gives existing members the right to buy shares from another member before he is allowed to sell them to a new member. Each share is equal in value. But that value may be greater or less than the nominal value. For example, a member of a successful company who bought shares at $10 each may be able to sell them at a premium—perhaps $12 each. But he may also find that he has to sell them for less than their nominal value—at a discount. Sometimes a company issues shares at a premium: for example, it sells $10 shares at $15 each.

Another way for a company to raise capital is by issuing **debentures**, or **bonds**, in return for loans. Debentureholders are entitled to an annual payment of interest, and this is not linked to the company's profits and losses. In general, they have the right to sell their debentures back to the company (that is, call in their loan), or sell them on to someone else. If possible, the lender will make sure his loan is secured by a charge over a company asset, so that he will have the right to take company property should there be no money to repay him.

A limited liability company is not the only way to run a business. A single person may operate as a sole trader, and even if he employs many people, he alone is responsible for management and, thus, for any debts. Another way to run a business is for two or more people to form a partnership in which they share management, profits, and liability to debts. The share is not necessarily an equal one, but depends upon the partnership agreement among them. This usually reflects the amount of capital each partner has invested in the business. Partnerships can be formed very easily and the legal position of partners is not very different from that of sole traders. Unlike members of a company, partners may find their personal property is at risk if they are sued by creditors. It is also possible to form an **unlimited company**. Since members' liability is unlimited this is, in effect, similar to a partnership.

If the advantage of forming a company is that it offers members some protection in case of bankruptcy, the disadvantage is that there are many regulations to observe in setting it up and running it. Under English law, there must be a minimum of two people, and they must sign a document called a **memorandum of association**, which must be filed with the national registrar of companies. The memorandum contains the name of the company, its objects, whether it is limited by shares or guarantee, and the amount of share capital. There are some restrictions on the choice of name: for example, the registrar will not accept a name that is the same or very similar to a company already registered, since this could confuse consumers and clients.

The objects clause of the memorandum is very important because a company may not engage in activity beyond its registered objects. Such activity is said to be **ultra vires**—outside its capacity. It used to be the case that both the company and its clients lost the right to remedies for breach of contract over an ultra vires transaction. The purpose of the doctrine was to stop company assets from being used for unauthorized activities. However, partly because of pressure to conform to European Community law, it is now possible for someone contracting with the company on ultra vires matters to be protected, provided the matter was authorized by the company's directors. In any case, companies usually draft very wide objects clauses to include any activities that the business is likely to be engaged in now or in the future.

As well as the memorandum, there are several other documents a new company has to register. When this has been done it receives a number and a certificate of incorporation and is ready to do business (unless it is a public limited company, in which case it must first obtain a trading certificate).

Internal management

The internal management of the company is regulated by a document called the **articles of association**. Although these need not be registered (except for companies limited by guarantee), they must conform to an authorized pattern. They detail rules about such matters as when and at what notice meetings must be held; members' voting rights, and the size of majority required to pass resolutions; issuing of shares; and the appointment, powers, and removal of directors. Under the Companies Act every public company must have at least two directors, and every private company, at least one. A director need not be a member (that is, a shareholder), but details of any shares he holds must be registered. He is not an employee of the company, but may be paid for his work as long as the members of the company agree to this. He has a duty to exercise a reasonable standard of care and not to make secret profits from company business. If he holds an interest in another firm with which the company is doing business, the law requires him to declare that interest at a board meeting (meeting of the directors).

The law also requires a limited company to keep accounting records at its registered office, including entries of receipts and payments and a record of assets and liabilities. These records must be open to inspection at any time by the company's directors and secretary, and a copy must be sent to the registrar each year. A profit and loss account, together with a financial report by the directors and a report from an independent auditor (inspector), must be put before a general meeting of the company's members every year. Breaking these regulations may result in criminal prosecution.

Another possible cause of criminal prosecution is **insider trading**. This means using inside knowledge to gain private profit when buying and selling company shares. Directors and employees of companies are often in a position to know if a company's shares are likely to rise or fall long before ordinary shareholders. As a result, they could make profits by buying or selling before everybody else, or by selling their special information. In 1990, a New York stockbroker was imprisoned for this offence. The crime was not even recognized in English law until 1967. The 1985 Company Securities (Insider Dealing) Act lays down a maximum penalty of two years imprisonment, but the recent discovery of how widespread this practice is means the penalty is likely to be increased as a deterrent.

Termination

There are several ways in which a company may be terminated (**dissolved**): its registration may be cancelled, as happened to Lindi St. Claire (Personal Services) Ltd. in 1980 because its objects turned out to be prostitution, which is illegal in Britain; it may be removed from the register if it has simply ceased to function as a company; or, it may be **liquidated**, or **wound up**. This means that its resources will be used to pay creditors in an established order of priority. It is likely that the reason the company is being wound up is that it is **bankrupt**—that is, it cannot pay all its debts. This mean that creditors may only get a proportion of what they are owed. As mentioned above, shareholders may be liable for up to the value of shares they hold but have not yet paid for. Sometimes liquidation is voluntary, at the insistence of most of the shareholders, and sometimes it is ordered by the court.

There are also laws regulating transactions in the years before liquidation. These laws prevent companies from transferring funds to third parties whom the creditors cannot touch before the firm goes bankrupt or from giving unauthorized preference to certain creditors.

Setting up, running, and winding down a company are not the only legal matters businessmen have to deal with. At some stage, most of them employ the services of lawyers for advice on how to minimize their tax liabilities and to make sure their business does not exceed noise or pollution regulations. Company directors, partners and sole traders alike have to consider the legal implications of making contracts to buy and supply goods and services, and the torts they may face if a product injures a consumer. More about consumers will be said in Chapter 13. In Chapter 14 legal obligations to the workforce will be discussed, and in Chapter 15, the protection of designs and inventions.

Running a business

Figure 11.1 *Lindi St. Clare, whose business was declared illegal in Britain.*

Running a business

Exercises

Comprehension
1 True or false?
   a A limited company may consist of one person only.
   b Limited companies cannot be sued.
   c The members of a limited company do not have to pay any company debts.
   d Companies can be forced to sell off all their assets in order to pay debts.
2 Describe two ways in which a business may raise money.
3 Name three forms in which a business may be run under English law.
4 What is an ultra vires transaction?
5 Name three ways in which a limited liability company may be dissolved.

Task
Using the contents section at the beginning of this book as a guide, list six areas of the law you think someone running a business needs to know about. After each item write a sentence explaining your choice.

12 The law and the family

In this chapter, we will look at how the law sees the family as a special institution; how some legal systems treat married couples and their children differently from the unmarried; the process of divorce; custody of and responsibility for children; and protection from violence in the home. Finally, we will consider the rights of succession to the property of a family member when they die.

Beyond the mere function of providing a new generation of children, the family is often promoted for its moral contribution to society. Despite a growing labor shortage, the Japanese government has passed very little legislation challenging the assumption that mothers should stay at home rather than go out to work. In Ireland, which is strongly influenced by the doctrines of the Catholic Church, divorce remains illegal.

In some societies the family is thought to be so important that there is very little legal intervention in family life. In many Islamic countries, for example, fathers, brothers and sons are allowed considerable authority over the females in their family. As late as the 1970s, the male head of the household in Switzerland was deemed to represent the interests of everyone within that household, and, consequently, none of the women could vote in national elections. But in many parts of the world, the law now promotes the rights of individuals within the family unit, and regulates family relations through legislation. Raised from the taxes of the working population as a whole, Child Benefit is paid directly to the mother, and retirement pensions are paid to grandparents, so that they are less dependent upon financial support from a family member. In Sweden, parents can be prosecuted for physically punishing their children and children have a limited capacity to divorce their parents. In Britain, as in many countries, there are special family courts with very strong powers to control and transfer private property in the interests of children. Much of the work of other courts is also directly relevant to family life.

Marriage law

The law in most countries places more emphasis upon marriages legally registered than social arrangements whereby people live together. In Japan, some couples prefer not to register their marriage because the law requires one of them to give up his or her name in favor of the other. The birth and residence documentation of children born to such marriages is different from that of other children and sometimes leads to discrimination. In Britain, children born outside legitimate marriages have fewer rights to financial support from estranged fathers than legitimate children. In addition, if they are born outside the UK, they are less likely than legitimate children to be granted British citizenship. Their fathers have no automatic right to have contact with them. Some welfare payments are calculated on a different basis according to whether recipients are married or not, and more procedures are available to a married woman than an unmarried one in seeking protection from domestic violence. However, in most industrialized countries, the legal differences between the married and the unmarried are decreasing. It is not surprising this should be the case in a nation like the United Sates, for example, here 25 percent of babies are now born to unmarried parents.

In English law, some marriages may be readily dissolved, or **nullified**—for example: if the couple never consummated the marriage, are blood relations, are under the legal age of sixteen (Pugh vs. Pugh, 1951) are both women (Talbot vs. Talbot, 1967), or, despite a surgical sex change, are both men (Corbett vs. Corbett, 1970). In other cases, a couple may seek a divorce. The procedure may be lengthy, especially if one spouse does not want to get divorced, or if there are children. In no case will English law allow divorce proceedings to start within a year of the marriage, since it is thought this is too soon for the marriage to have tested itself. It is also feared that people would get married without serious thought if it were quick and easy to get a divorce.

Divorce law

Divorce proceedings in England take place in certain County Courts known as divorce county courts. Some matters are also dealt with in the Family Division of the High Court. It is necessary for one of the parties to convince the court that the marriage has broken down irretrievably—without any chance of reconciliation. To do this the person seeking, or **petitioning for** divorce, must prove one of five things: that the other party, or **respondent**, committed adultery (had sex with someone else); that the respondent's behavior has been unreasonable; that the respondent deserted the petitioner at least two years previously; that the couple has lived apart for two years and both agree to a divorce; or that they have lived apart for five years. Even if the court is satisfied that there is enough evidence of one of the above, a divorce will not be issued until satisfactory arrangements have been made for any children of the marriage, including determining who is to have **custody** of the children, the rights of the

Law and the family

Figure 12.1 *The wedding... and after.*

children to maintain contact with the other parent, and financial arrangement for the children's welfare.

The High Court or divorce county court has wide powers to order both an ex-husband and an ex-wife to make financial provisions for the other and for their children. This may include periodic payments, a lump sum of cash, transfer of property into the other spouse's name, or sale of property so that the money can be divided. In general, these orders are supposed to support the children and other spouse (usually the one taking care of the children; often the mother) until they become financially independent.

When a couple separates, whether married or unmarried, the welfare of any children and the division of any property are the most important, and often the most difficult problems, to resolve. People who once lived together happily may argue bitterly once the trust between them has dissolved. Although it is possible, and certainly much cheaper, to arrange most of the terms of a divorce privately without lawyers, many couples find that it is impossible for them to reach such an agreement.

In the case of property, the courts have to find a balance between two principles. One is that any division should fairly reflect how much each party contributed to the property they held together. In the past, some women suffered when they separated from their husband because the house they lived in was bought with his money and registered in his name. Nowadays, courts look beyond legal ownership and cash contributions. Work done in the home, time spent caring for the family, even emotional support, are all considered as giving some rights to property. In the United States, there have been cases of the lovers of famous entertainers claiming a proportion of the income earned by their partner during the time they lived together, and sometimes millions of dollars have been at issue. When Cindy Nelson separated from her girlfriend, tennis star Martina Navratilova, she produced a contract that the two women had signed when they lived together to support her huge claim for money.

The other principle which courts must consider is the needs of the parties. It is no longer assumed that a woman who was financially dependent on her husband when they were married will remain so after they are divorced, but the length of the marriage and the age and skills of the woman will be considered in deciding how soon—if at all—she is likely to become independent. There are a few cases of a court refusing to grant a divorce at all because the couple in question was elderly and would never recover from the financial shock.

Protection of children

In general, the welfare of children is the biggest concern of family law. Virtually all societies, and certainly all legal systems, treat children differently from adults. There are special courts to deal with young people who commit crimes (see Chapter 4). In economically developed countries, there are limits on the type and amount of work a child is allowed to do. There are age limits on the rights and duties of citizens; however, these vary from country to country. A Japanese may not vote until he is twenty, but a German may vote at eighteen. A Briton may marry at sixteen with his parents' consent, or at eighteen without it; a French girl may marry at fourteen, but a boy must wait until he is sixteen. In some parts of the United States you may drive a car at fifteen, but in others, not until eighteen. It is interesting that in many places a person may be sentenced to death at an age when he is not allowed to vote. Parents have a duty to make decisions, for example those concerning education, on behalf of their children. When parents are dead or absent, a legal **guardian** is appointed to make these decisions. Sometimes this is an adoptive parent—a person who legally adopts the child as his or her own and has all the rights and duties of a natural parent. Sometimes, it is a local authority, as in the case of children who have been taken into care because their parents are ill, in prison or unable to take care of them.

Rights of succession

An important event for a family, usually requiring consultation with a lawyer, is the death of a relative. The property of a dead person is mostly dealt with in Anglo-American law under the law of **probate**. This is distinct from family law and of course it is not only relatives who may receive (**inherit**) the property of a dead person. However, it seems appropriate to consider Probate in a chapter about family law since it is usually family members who are concerned with registering the death, paying the dead person's debts and tax liabilities, and acquiring his property.

Many people make a **will** before their death containing their instructions regarding what is to happen to their property when they die. In English law, the maker of a will is called a **testator**. The will need not be drawn up by a lawyer, but there are certain regulations about how it must be made. For example, it must be in writing, and there must be two witnesses who sign the will (see the document at the end of Chapter 5). Clearly such requirements are necessary since once the testator is dead, no one can ask him to explain his intentions. The testator may give away all of his property (his **estate**), both real and personal. He need not give it to a family member. However, under the 1975 Inheritance (Provision for Family and Dependants) Act, English courts have some powers to modify the will if it is unfair to a spouse, child or other dependent.

A will can be quite a simple document. Yet many people never make one—they die **intestate**. Sometimes this is because of carelessness. But often it is simply because they do not have a great deal of property and believe it is clear who will inherit that property after their death. In most countries, there are **laws of succession** which clearly lay down who is entitled to the property of an intestate relative and in what order. Under English law, a surviving spouse is at the top of this order, followed by children, parents, brothers and sisters, grandparents and uncles, aunts and cousins. If there are no relatives at all the property passes to the State, but it is likely that the court will make some provision for any non-relative who had been a dependent of the dead person.

In the French Civil Code, as well as under a will or the laws of succession, property may be passed by a contract made with another person to come into effect on death, although this is unusual. In English law as well, the people administering the property of a dead person may need to consider contracts he had made. Actions in both contract and tort may be made against the estate of a person even after he has died. If a contract was in the process of being made at the time of death the law may have some difficulty in deciding if it is valid or not. The English case of Bradbury vs. Morgan (1862) suggests that an offer may be accepted (and therefore a contract made: see Chapter 6) even after the death of the offeror.

Whether there is a will or not, it may take some time to deal with the dead person's property. It is necessary to work out how much property there is; whether there are debts to be paid; whether a trust needs to be set up for gifts to children (see Chapter 9); and whether someone entitled to property prefers not to take it—for example, a business which is more trouble to run than it is worth. Sometimes there is **partial intestacy**: there is a will dealing with some of the dead person's property, but not all of it. In this case, both the terms of the will and the laws of succession need to be applied. And there may be Inheritance Tax to pay (unless the property is under a certain value or all of it is to pass to the dead person's spouse).

Exercises

Comprehension
1 Give examples from different countries of how the family is given special legal consideration.
2 Describe four ways in which UK laws favor marriage over unmarried relationships.
3 True or false under English law?
   a Divorce may not be granted within a year of marriage.
   b After two years of living apart a couple may get divorced, even if one of them objects.
   c A divorce may be arranged without a lawyer.
4 What are the two principles an English Court considers when dividing family property during a divorce?
5 Suggest two reasons why most people don't make a will.

Task
Make a list of age limits in your country for such activities as marriage, voting, driving a car, smoking. Now conduct a survey of others in the class to find out their opinion as to whether the limits are too high or low. Record their answers.

13 The law and consumers

Suppose you are buying a television set. Can you be sure that the set you take home will be of the same type and quality as the one you have looked at in the store? If the TV breaks down after you have bought it, who should pay for the repair—you, the shop or the manufacturer? What should you do if you are not satisfied with the repair or with the fee that the engineer charges? If you are very unlucky and the set catches fire, who should pay for any damage to your house? These are questions of consumer law.

Anyone who buys goods or services, whether an individual shopper or a large business, is a **consumer**. However, consumer law is mostly concerned with the rights of private individuals. Consumer rights are not a new concept. Pre-industrial societies throughout the world have imposed punishments on traders who overcharge or otherwise deceive their customers, even if they make honest mistakes. Bakers in Medieval England were so worried about the laws against selling underweight bread that they developed the custom of adding an extra roll free to a batch of twelve. Even today the expression "a baker's dozen" means thirteen of something, not twelve.

In the last thirty years, consumer law has grown at an unprecedented rate and is often studied as a branch of law in its own right. The principles of contract and tort are particularly relevant to consumer matters, but in addition to these, new legislation is passed every year to clarify the law and deal with specific problems.

Not surprisingly, consumer law has grown most quickly in wealthier industrialized countries where people are accustomed to asserting their rights and have a wide range of information available to them. In Britain, the magazine *Which?* has been publishing independently researched information about products, services and legal rights for thirty years, and popular television programs discuss consumer complaints. If a discontented consumer is forced to take legal action, there are judicial institutions which enable him or her to do this without spending a lot of money. In developing countries where manufacturers often have low profit margins, consumers often have to accept lower standards unless they are rich or have important friends. But there are changes here, too. The Chinese government, for example, has responded to a growing demand for better quality goods by setting up special courts to deal with complaints.

Contracts

A lot of consumer law is basic contract law. The consumer must show that he had a contract with the supplier of goods or services, show that the supplier is in breach of this agreement, and convince the supplier that he would have a good chance of winning if he took the case to court. As mentioned in Chapter 6, contracts between businesses are usually full of detailed agreements about who should supply what, when, where and at what price, but everyday transactions involving private individuals are more informal. Very little is written down or even spoken, and the consumer must show that a contract has been implied by law. To help him there are consumer laws implying certain terms into consumer agreements.

Figure 13.1 *Consumer law is growing to keep pace with consumerism.*

In English law, for example, the 1979 Sale of Goods Act implies a term that the seller has a right to sell. This protects the honest buyer from a seller who had no right to sell goods because they had been stolen. Another implied term is that goods correspond to any description given to the buyer. Another is that they be of "merchantable quality"—but this only applies if the seller is in business. When buying from a private seller the buyer may have to rely on express terms about quality. The 1982 Supply of Goods and Services Act implies similar terms regarding services. It also implies that services be provided with reasonable care at a reasonable cost and within a reasonable time. In deciding what is reasonable an English court will refer to similar previous cases. However, the most important guideline is usually common sense in the context of the transaction in question.

Where goods are concerned, the implied terms are **conditions**. This means that the buyer has the right to **discharge** the contract—to refuse the goods—if the terms are breached. He may also be entitled to damages (see Chapter 6). But where services are concerned, the implied terms are **intermediate stipulations**. This means that the consumer may only refuse the services if this is reasonable in the circumstances. The court may decide that he must accept work which has been done, but award him damages where the work has been done badly or too slowly or at too high a cost.

A difficult problem in consumer law is deciding who is responsible when goods are lost in delivery or delivered late. If no express agreement has been made about this, the Sale of Goods Act provides complicated rules. In general, the buyer has no responsibility until the time he takes possession of the goods. If goods arrive late he may be able to discharge the contract (refuse delivery) if he can show that time was of the essence (of vital importance). Sometimes this is implied by the nature of the transaction— for example, a contract to deliver fresh food or newspapers. In other cases, the consumer may make time of the essence by specifying a time for delivery. In the 1950 case of Richards vs. Oppenheimer, the buyer of a car continued to ask for delivery even after the date in the contract had passed. This implied that he had given up (waived) his right to discharge the contract for late delivery. However, he then gave the supplier another 30 days to deliver. Time was once again of the essence and when the car was finally delivered more than 30 days later the buyer was entitled to refuse the car and to refuse to pay any money.

Exemptions

Another difficult problem is that of **exemption clauses**. These are warnings to the consumer by the supplier that no responsibility will be accepted in the case of loss, damage or injury. For example, dry-cleaning businesses often have notices on a wall or on the back of tickets refusing responsibility for damage to clothes. Parking lots have sign saying that customers park at their own risk. Sports clubs warn that they are not liable if members injure themselves using their equipment. The law about exemption clauses varies from country to country, but in general it is important for the consumer to know that not all such clauses are valid. In Britain and the United States, for example, a party trying to avoid responsibility must show that the exemption clause was part of the contract with the customer and that it covered the problem in question.

The clause is more likely to be part of the contract if it is in a document signed by the customer or was written in a place all customers could read it. However, in the 1964 Scottish case of MacCutcheon vs. MacBrayne, a ferry company was unable to rely on a notice on a wall because it normally also asked customers to sign a form warning about risks of damage and injury but had failed to do so in the case of Mr. MacCutcheon. The 1977 Unfair Contract Terms Act makes it illegal for a business in Britain to try to limit responsibility for death or personal injury resulting from negligence. Responsibility for loss or damage or loss can only be avoided if this would be deemed reasonable.

Product liability

One of the fastest-growing areas of consumer law is **product liability**—responsibility for damage or injury caused by faulty goods. During the 1960s, a series of cases in the United States established the principle that consumers need only to show damage, effect, and a relation between the two. In 1985, the European Community issued a directive setting similar standards leading to new laws in seven EC countries, such as the 1987 Consumer Protection Act in Britain. Before this directive, British consumers had to pursue an action in the tort of negligence (see Chapter 8). The new law simplifies the requirements of proof and allows action against the supplier and importer as well as the manufacturer. In Japan, consumers still have to prove not only that there was a defect leading to damage, but that this was a result of the producer's clear negligence. Consumers complain that it is extremely difficult for them to win cases, partly because rules of technological secrets allow companies to withhold important information about products.

But there are some people who think things have gone too far in America, where there are thousands of new cases every year (compared with 130 in the last fifteen years in Japan). American manufacturers complain that they have to raise prices because of increased insurance bills to cover legal cases. There have even been attempts to extend product liability beyond manufactured goods to movies, television programs and music. Defendants in criminal cases have tried to use the defence that their actions were the result of being influenced by something they saw on television. In 1988, parents sued rock star Ozzy Osbourne after their child killed himself; they claimed that he had been influenced by song lyrics. They lost the case, but the judge said that the principle of freedom of speech did not necessarily exempt rock stars from legal responsibility in such cases.

The law and consumers

Another problem manufacturers now have to worry about is what to do when someone threatens to put poison or glass or some other harmful substance in a product to be consumed by the public. In Japan, organized crime associations and individual employees have often used such threats in order to get money from a company. Even when the company could find no evidence of the threat having been carried out, it has usually decided to pay the money rather than take the risk of losing its sales. But what happens if a company refuses to be threatened, leaves its products on the shelves, and a member of the public is consequently poisoned? In the United States the Food and Drug Administration has laid down guidelines for companies depending on the likelihood of harm to the public.

One of the difficulties for governments when they make consumer legislation is to balance the interest of the consumer against those of the producer. In Britain, food shoppers sometimes complain that they are underprotected because their interests are looked after by the same government ministry that looks after the interests of the farming and fishing industry. On the other hand, in the last 25 years, the government has passed legislation about description of goods, consumer credit, unsafe goods, and many other things in addition to the laws mentioned above. Citizen's Advice Bureaus give free advice not only about products but also about welfare benefits, health services, educational and other public services. There is a danger that consumer law is becoming so broad it is difficult to define what it is.

Exercises

Comprehension
1 Compare consumer law in developed and develping countries.
2 In English Law, after a breach of contract a consumer may refuse goods more easily than services. Why do you think the law makes this difference?
3 True or false in English law?
   a If delivery is late a consumer may always refuse goods.
   b Seller and buyer have equal responsibility if goods are lost before delivery.
   c Exemption clauses have no legal force.
4 Compare Japanese and American product liability law.
5 What is a Citizen's Advice Bureau?

Discussion
"People should have the right to sue TV companies showing programs that may have a harmful influence on viewers."
Write a paragraph containing two arguments for and two against this statement. Then discuss your answer with other students.

14 Employment law

Like consumer law, employment law is a very large topic in which the principles of tort and contract have been greatly added to by specific legislation. The history of employment law really begins with the industrialization of Western countries in the 19th century. Before industrialization most people worked on the land or in some craft connected with agriculture. They tended to work for the same employer in the same place most of their life. Employment rights depended upon paternalistic employers and informal agreements. Many employees were in a very weak position because part of their wages was paid in the form of food and accommodation. Although there were peasant movements which succeeded in improving conditions—over 1,000 of them in Tokugawa Japan, for example—few of them led to legislation or outlasted the protest in question.

Industrialization brought large numbers of workers together in the same workplace. Recognizing their strength in times of economic expansion and their weakness during depressions, they began to organize themselves more systematically than farmworkers. In response, governments began to see a need for legislation in order to standardize rights and conditions. Laws were passed to recognize and also limit the right of workers to strike. Other legislation dealt with health and safety in the workplace, and limits upon working hours and ages. Toward the end of the century, Germany and other countries developed systems of insurance to protect workers during sickness, unemployment and retirement.

The 20th century has seen a great increase in the detail of such legislation. Although employees' rights seem to have expanded during labor shortages (as in present-day Japan) and contracted in times of unemployment, there has been a steady increase in the areas of employment that the law has come to regulate. Most of the richer countries now have legislation which guarantees a minimum wage for all workers; prevents employees from being dismissed without some reason, period of advance notice, or compensation; and requires employers to give their employees a written statement of the main term of their employment contract. In the last twenty years, many countries have also passed laws to ensure that men and women are given equal opportunities to do the same work in the same conditions.

Employment rights

English law makes a clear distinction between employees and self-employed people. In general, employees have far more legal rights because they are thought to be in a weaker economic position than the self-employed. For example, the 1978 Employment Protection (Consolidation) Act requires that employees be given a written summary of their conditions of work; it provides that employees be given at least a week's notice if employment is to be ended; and it gives employees the right to compensation if they are dismissed unfairly or made redundant (dismissed because there is no longer any suitable work). This same Act also gives women the right to time off in order to have a baby and the right to return to work within a certain period after having the baby. The application of these rights, however, depends upon the circumstances of employment. For example, people who work part-time (under 16 hours a week) have little protection. Men over 65 and women over 60 are not entitled to compensation for redundancy. The Unfair Dismissal Tribunal sometimes rules that it is fair for an employer to dismiss a sick employee, especially if the employer is a small business. And companies employing fewer than five people do not have to re-employ a woman who leaves to have a baby.

Other English legislation, such as the 1970 Equal Pay Act, the 1976 Race Relations Act, and the 1975 and 1986 Sex Discrimination Acts, attempts to ensure equality of opportunity for employees and job applicants whatever their race or sex. People complaining of discrimination have the right to take their case to an industrial tribunal. Julie Hayward, a cook at a shipyard in Scotland, claimed that it was unfair that male painters, engineers and carpenters at her workplace were paid more than she was. Since the Equal Pay Act requires equal pay for work of equal value, the industrial tribunal carried out a job evaluation survey. The case was finally decided in her favor by the House of Lords. Mrs. Ursula Hurley won her claim against unfair dismissal after her employer dismissed her because he thought a woman should stay at home to look after her young children. A male worker won his claim that he should not have to work in a very dirty part of a factory because women were not required to work there.

EC employment law

EC law sometimes gives better protection to employees than English law. When Ms. Helen Marshall claimed that she should not have been made to retire from her job at age 62 since male employees were allowed to continue until they were 65, she lost her case at an industrial tribunal which argued that EC law did not prevent member countries from having different retirement ages for men and women. But the European Court ruled that although different ages for receiving retirement pension were legal, it was not legal for a member state to force women to retire from work earlier than men.

Since there is supposed to be a single labor market in the EC there have been many attempts to harmonize employment rights among member states. One of the many questions still to be agreed on is whether there should be a standard minimum wage. Supporters argue that low-paid workers would be better protected if all employers had to pay a minimum hourly rate. But opponents say that this would put too much pressure on small businesses and discourage them from creating new jobs.

Sunday trading is another issue dividing the EC. Although many European countries allow businesses to open every day of the week, the 1950 Shops Act limits Sunday trading in Britain—partly for religious reasons, and partly to ensure that shopworkers get at least one day's holiday a week. But the rules are complicated and out of date. Stores can sell whiskey, for example, but not coffee; magazines but not books; lightbulbs for cars but not for houses. Some fish and chip shops can sell many kinds of takeaway food on Sundays, but not fish and chips. B & Q, a large D-I-Y business, has claimed that the 1950 Act restricts imports from other EC countries and, therefore, breaks Article 30 of the Treaty of Rome.

The right to strike was one of the first employment rights to be recognized by law, yet the specific rules have varied from time to time and country to country. Since the 1984 Trade Union Act, all strikes in Britain must be supported by a majority vote of the workers in a secret ballot. Technically, strike action still constitutes a breach of an employee's contract of employment. Indeed in 1976 when Grunwick, a London film-processing firm, dismissed all its striking workers, the workers lost their claim in an industrial tribunal for unfair dismissal. However, employers are unlikely to dismiss worker who are all backed by a trade union. When Britain had a high record of strikes in the 1970s, it was sometimes said that there were too many different unions inside each company—one to represent each kind of job. Recently there has been a trend towards adopting single-union agreements whether it is legal for an employer to decide which union a worker is to join.

Comparison with Japan

There are fewer employment laws in Japan than in many Western countries. Few workers are given clear job descriptions or written

Employment law

Figure 14.1 *The right to strike: an employment right recognised by law.*

contracts and it is unusual for an employee to take legal action against his employer. The main law about sexual discrimination simply asks employers to make efforts to reduce discrimination, without imposing clear duties or penalties. However, as in other aspects of Japanese society, it is not clear if the low level of legal activity necessarily means that employees have fewer rights. It certainly seems to be the case that workers have to work very long hours and often do not ask for overtime payment. Despite the current labor shortage, which has encouraged employers to hire women to do more responsible and better paid work than before, very few women enjoy equal employment opportunities. In addition, many jobs remain closed to workers of non-Japanese origin, even those who have lived all their lives in Japan. On the other hand, Japanese workers enjoy more security than many employees in western countries. Once hired, they are unlikely to be dismissed. Insurance benefits and recreational facilities are usually made available to them by their companies, and many workers are able to live in big cities only because their employers provide low-cost accommodation for them.

One legal development in Japan which has yet to spread to western countries is law suits against the employers of workers who had died of *karoushi*—not a specific accident in the workplace or industrial-related disease, but general stress brought about by overwork. In 1992, the widow of a Mitsui Company employee was awarded ¥30 million in compensation after a court learned that her husband had been spending 103 days a year away from home on stressful business trips before his sudden death.

Exercises

Comprehension
1 List eight employee rights which have developed in industrialized countries.
2 True or false?
   a Small companies in Britain need not rehire an employee who leaves to have a baby.
   b EC law is of no benefit to workers in Britain.
   c All EC workers have minimum wage laws.
   d Striking workers cannot be dismissed in Britain if a majority of them have agreed to the strike in a secret vote.
3 What disadvantages do many Japanese workers face?
4 What benefits do many Japanese workers enjoy?

Discussion
"People should be free to work and trade on Sunday, just as any other day."
Write a paragraph containing two arguments for and two against this statement. Then discuss your answer with other students.

15   Intellectual property

Patents and copyrights

In general, it is not against the law to steal someone else's ideas. If a man I meet in a bar tells me how people can become rich, and I publish a best-selling book based on his ideas, I do not have to pay him any money or even mention his name in the book. But most countries do place legal limits on copying the exact words someone has written, the art or music they have created, or the technology they have invented. Such work is known as **intellectual property**. The main legal instruments for protecting it are **patents** and **copyrights**.

In order to prevent a new discovery or scientific process from being copied, it is necessary to apply for a patent. If granted, a patent makes it illegal for others to manufacture or use the invention without permission. However, a patent will only be granted if the invention has not yet been shown in public and if it has industrial application. Ideas—mathematical and scientific theories, for example—cannot be patented. The patent must be carefully worded since it may be possible for someone to copy any part of the process or invention not mentioned in the patent.

Literature, artistic works, computer programs, movies and radio and television broadcasts cannot be patented, but they can be protected by copyright. In most countries, such work is automatically protected when it is created; there is no need to apply for or to register copyright. It is usual to record the date of creation and mark it with the international copyright symbol ©, but this is not essential.

As with other kinds of property, intellectual property can only be protected if ownership is clear. The holder of a patent is often a company rather than the individual scientists inventing something in the course of their work. A copyright is usually owned by the creator of the work—the writer, painter or musician—but like other property, it might be passed to someone else. If a journalist is employed by a newspaper then the articles he writes are usually the copyright of the newspaper owner. The copyright in a movie is owned by the film maker, not by individual writers or performers. The copyright in this book is held by the publishers who commissioned it.

Keeping pace with technology

In recent years it has been difficult for intellectual property law to keep pace with technological change. Video recording, satellite television, and the use of computers have expanded so rapidly that it is becoming difficult to control copying. The main emphasis of recent laws is not to prevent people from copying, but to ensure they pay for doing so.

In Britain, the 1988 Copyright, Designs and Patents Act covers a work of music, art, drama or literature, computer software, for 50 years after the author's death; sound recordings, films, and broadcasts for 50 years after they are made or broadcast; and other writings for 25 years after publication. In theory, the law applies to copying done anywhere in the world. To increase the likelihood of enforcing intellectual property law internationally, there are several important international conventions such as the Universal Copyright Convention, the Bern Convention, and the Patent Corporation Treaty. Whether a country signs and tries to enforce such agreements usually depends upon whether it is likely to gain from the agreement. Poorer countries usually produce fewer inventions and new works of art and literature than richer ones. Consequently, they are more interested in the benefits of copying than the problems of being copied.

The laws of intellectual property usually require anyone wanting to copy something to ask permission from the holder of the patent or copyright. In the case of small-scale use of artistic work, permission is often granted free of charge. For industrial use of a scientific invention, a great deal of money might need to be paid. But most legal systems allow a certain amount of copying even without asking permission.

For example, under the 1988 Act, a play may be performed in private—for example, at a school—a long as there is no audience from outside and no one is asked for money to watch. A television program may be recorded only if it is done so that it can be watched at home at a more convenient time. However, it is illegal to tape a record, even if this is for private listening. The concept of **fair dealing** allows someone to make a photocopy of someone else's work as long as this is done for private study and no more than a substantial part of the book or article is copied. But it is not legal to make a large number of copies, for example, for a whole class of students.

Trademarks and trade secrets

Another kind of intellectual property is a **trademark**. Companies often use a certain name or description to help sell their products, or sometimes a symbol which everyone comes to associate with that company, such as the

M design of McDonald's or the shell design of Shell Oil. To prevent other businesses from using their trademark, companies often register them. Another legal remedy is to take out an injunction against a company which has tried to pass itself off as your company by using the same name or similar packaging. The London store Harrod's took out a passing-off action against a small business in New Zealand not only because it was also called Harrod's but because its bags looked similar.

The law provides some help for companies that want to keep trade secrets confidential. In some countries, it is a criminal offense to pass information about an employer's production methods, business techniques and customer lists. In others, it is legal for a contract of employment to include restrictions about giving away or using such secrets, and the restrictions may continue to apply even after the employee has left the company. Some contracts enable a company to take legal action against an ex-employee who tries to work for a competitor. English law recognizes the need for businesses to protect themselves from ex-employees who start up a rival business, but it also puts limits upon the extent that the company can restrict others.

Enforcement is a major problem in intellectual property law. In some case, infringing copyright can be a criminal offense. For example, filming or recording a live performance without permission and for commercial purposes can result under English law in imprisonment for two years and a £2000 fine. But if the filming or recording is made for private purposes, the performer will have to take out a civil action in order to obtain an injunction or compensation. Copyright holders usually take a practical approach; it would be a waste of time and money to sue every individual who makes a private recording of music. In Germany the price of tape recorders and video recorders includes a fee paid to the Musicians Union and other associations of people likely to suffer from unauthorized copying. Japan has long been criticized by Western countries for not respecting intellectual property rights. Video and CD rental stores even sell blank tapes! But the government agreed in 1992 to put an extra charge on blank tapes to be collected by recording companies.

Exercises

Comprehension
1 What is the difference between a patent and a copyright?
2 Why has technological change caused problems for intellectual property law?
3 Why are developed countries more likely than developing ones to sign international intellectual property agreements?
4 True or false?
   a Copyrighted property cannot be copied.
   b Copyrighted property can only be copied if money is paid.
   c Some property can be copied even without asking permission.

Discussion
"Copying audio and video tapes at home is just as bad as stealing them from a store."

Write a paragraph containing two arguments for and two against this statement. Then discuss your answer with other students.

Part Four
Law, Politics and Society

16 Freedom of speech and expression

In 1988, Penguin Books published *The Satanic Verses*, a novel by the Indian-born British writer Salman Rushdie. Many Muslims found the book offensive to their religion, and, by the end of the year, Saudi Arabia, India, Pakistan, Egypt, Somalia, Sudan, Malaysia, Qatar, Indonesia and South Africa had all forbidden its publication in their countries. A campaign began to ban the book in Britain. The Islamic Foundation called for prosecution under the UK laws against **blasphemy**—denial of or insults against God. But the government argued that this rarely-applied law refers in Britain only to the Christian religion.

The issue of *The Satanic Verses* encouraged a debate about freedom of speech which continues today. Rushdie himself lives in hiding because the late Ayatollah Khomeini of Iran called for his death, and Iranian authorities offered a reward to anyone who killed him. The French government argued that Rushdie had the right to publish his book, that no one had the right to call for his death and withdrew diplomats from Iran. Some prominent people in Britain called for greater understanding of the religion and culture of minority ethnic groups, arguing that the blasphemy laws there should be extended to cover all religions. Others argued that we should tolerate someone else's views even if they attack our deepest beliefs and called for the abolition of the blasphemy laws altogether.

The consultation of almost every country guarantees freedom of speech. In practice, however, every government puts legal limits on what its citizens may say, as well as on what they may write, the films they may make, and even on the pictures they may paint. Why is this?

Political censorship

Despite the English saying, "Sticks and stones may break my bones but names can never hurt me," many people feel that words can hurt and need to be controlled just as actions do. The extent to which free expression is

Freedom of speech and expression

Figure 16.1 *Burning* The Satanic Verses: *testing the right to freedom of speech and expression.*

controlled varies greatly from country to country.

At one end of the scale, in some countries, the law bans the expression of any ideas that are against the interests of the State. This may mean any criticism of government policy or government officials. This used to be typical of many of the socialist countries of Eastern Europe before 1989. In Romania, for example, all public meetings had to be authorized in advance and criticism of the government was punishable by imprisonment. All schools and colleges were tightly controlled. Both teacher and staff risked expulsion if their ideas were unorthodox. In Bulgaria, the Turkish minority was not allowed to use Turkish names; the content of all newspapers had to be approved and sometimes changed (**censored**) before publication; and artists were allowed to paint and write only works that "served the people." In the former Czechoslovakia, all radio and television networks were owned and controlled by the state, and private individuals were not allowed to own photocopiers in case they distributed "unauthorized" ideas. Similar restrictions still exist in other parts of the world. In North Korea, for example, it is a crime to listen to a foreign radio station, to write a satirical play or to play Western music. In Ethiopia, all journalists must be state employees.

Many governments admit that they restrict expression but justify their actions as being in the interest of the majority of the people. In answer to criticisms of its human rights policies, the Chinese government argues that freedom to say and write anything at all is not as important a freedom as economic well-being, and the former must be restricted in favor of the latter. The Taiwanese government has claimed that the special position of their island country next to the Chinese mainland as the home of the true government of the whole of China justifies the existence of the death penalty for anyone who argues in favor of Taiwanese independence. In practice, however, calls for independence are now commonly made.

Governments often restrict information in the interests of national security. Passing military secrets to a foreign government, for example, may bring prosecution for **treason**—the crime of trying to betray or overthrow a state (which in Britain is still theoretically punishable by death, unlike murder). Some people have criticized the British Official Secrets Act, which can be used to restrict information about government dealings even when there is no risk to national security. For example, in 1988 the act was used to ban publication of *Spycatcher*, a book about the intelligence services written in breach of his duty of confidentiality by a retired member of the secret services. The book was considered harmless, and, in any case, could be bought legally in many foreign countries.

Every country controls its news reporting when it is at war, even if it admits this is an unfortunate necessity. During the Falklands campaign in 1982, the BBC, which takes pride in its reputation for independent reporting, was not allowed to report certain facts about the war while it was taking place. South Korea is still technically in a state of war with the North, and, therefore, the South Korean government does not tolerate views sympathetic to the North.

It is interesting that the countries which restrict freedom of expression least tend to be those which are the most economically developed. But it would be wrong to think that free speech is the privilege only of rich countries; Costa Rica, for example, with a per capita GDP of only just over $1,000, allows considerable freedom to its journalists, writers, artists and teachers, whereas Singapore (GNP $16,000) requires annual licenses for journals, has a three-year jail penalty for seditious tendencies, and sometimes bans foreign publications critical of the government.

Some governments see freedom of speech as a basic human right and take pride in their own tolerance of different forms of expression, even when these forms are critical of them; clearly, Swedes, Canadians and Japanese have more freedom to say what they want than Chinese or South Africans. Nevertheless, restrictions exist even in apparently liberal countries, and it is interesting to consider what purpose these serve.

Words of violence and racism

Most societies prohibit speech and writing which they think will directly provoke physical violence or other illegal behavior. In January 1992, Mark Hopkins was executed in Wyoming for telling others to murder four people. In such a case, perhaps it is not so much that the words are illegal as that the person who gives the orders is just as guilty as the one who does the killing. But "threats to kill" and "threatening behavior" are examples of crimes in which the words themselves are illegal, whether or not they lead to an act. The latter, not part of the 1986 Public Order Act in Britain, outlaws threatening, abusive or insulting words (as well as behavior) which are likely to cause another to believe that immediate violence will occur. Most people accept the need for such limitations on speech; however, there is a danger of inhibiting a protestor who holds peaceful views and expresses them peacefully but knows that certain people will react violently to them.

More controversial is the area in which people hold political beliefs that involve violence. Some governments attempt to tolerate the opinions of any political groups but not the direct advocacy of violence. In Spain, where the paramilitary group ETA is seeking independence for the Basques, Basque nationalists may sit in parliament, but it is illegal to encourage "pro-terrorist sentiments." In Britain, membership in the Irish Republican Army (IRA) is illegal, but membership in its political wing, Sinn Fein, is not. In 1989, the British government tried to restrict Sinn Fein's publicity; its spokesmen were allowed to appear on television, but their views regarding the overthrow of British rule in Ireland could not be expressed in their own voices—written words, or another person's voice, had to be substituted. Amnesty International campaigns for the release of people imprisoned because of their opinions—as long as they have not advocated violence.

Another disputed area is censorship of views that discriminate against specific groups in society, especially on the grounds of race or sex. In Britain, it is a crime to "incite racial hatred." In many ways, this is similar to the legislation against threatening words, referring to situations in which members of a racial minority are subjected to verbal abuse. But legislation to prevent racial discrimination also goes beyond this. Advertisements for jobs cannot specify race. Racist views may be banned from television and radio. In January 1993, an historian was fined by a German court for calling into question the number of Jews who died in concentration camps during World War II. And a 1972 French law against racism permits the banning of newspaper articles which provoke discrimination. While many people welcome such legislation, there are others who feel all views, even disagreeable ones, have the right to be heard.

Art, literature and pornography

In addition to controls on political and religious ideas, almost every country attempts to control art and culture. Policies seem to range widely from country to country. In the 1970s, a picture by the artist Gempei Akasegawa was banned in Japan because it incorporated a very realistic copy of a ¥1,000 note—technically the crime of forging (copying) bank notes! Visitors to Japan from Scandinavia, where sex scenes are permissible in the media (but violence is controlled) are surprised to learn that very violent films and comic books are widely available, yet nudity is so heavily censored that a picture in a *Time* magazine of a woman breastfeeding her baby was blanked out.

In many countries there is great debate as to whether pornographic or violent material encourages criminal behavior. Some convicted rapists have been found to have read magazines depicting violent sex scenes. On the other hand, Japanese society appears to be relatively non-violent despite the availability of violent literature. It has been argued that sex and violence are two different forms of behavior and, to avoid association between the two, violence should be discouraged, not sex. People have a variety of motives for seeking censorship, and they are not all conservative. Both conservative and radical women's groups in Britain and America have complained about pictures of nude women in daily newspapers. This is not necessarily because they feel such pictures increase sexual assaults against women (although many feel that they do); some object to the growth of free sexual behavior in society altogether. Others have liberal views on sex but believe such pictures encourage the attitude that women are passive sex objects rather than active and independent individuals.

Few legal systems clearly specify what kind of literary and pictorial expression is acceptable. (Although in Japan a rather rigid law banning "pubic hair" was made, apparently because the lawmakers did not want to use the word "genitals," and this has been interpreted literally). In general governments lay down certain guidelines and apply them according to their own views or the apparent opinion of the majority of the public. The important question behind all of this seems not to be what is and isn't harmful for us, but rather, to what extent governments should make these decisions for their citizens.

Defamation

Most of the above issues have been matters of public (constitutional or criminal) law. There are also restrictions upon speech in civil law. If a person feels that someone has said something about him which is not only untrue but has seriously harmed his reputation, he may sue that person in the tort of **defamation**. In Anglo-American law this is known as **slander** if the words were spoken, **libel** if they were written. Journalists and other writers have to be particularly careful to check their facts before publishing. If the case is proven, the defendant is ordered to pay damages to the plaintiff. In the case of some famous entertainers or public figures the amount of money has sometimes been very high. Sometimes a high award is made against a newspaper as **punitive damages** if the court feels that the newspaper knew it was printing something defamatory but went ahead and did so in the belief it would increase its readership and thus its profits. Some people in Britain feel that the laws of defamation do not provide enough protection for ordinary people who may not be able to afford to sue a newspaper or television company. Others believe the media should be free to print stories without the fear of a libel action every time they make a mistake.

Exercises

Comprehension

1. After *The Satanic Verses* controversy, what two contrasting suggestions were made for changing Britain's blasphemy laws?
2. Briefly list restrictions on speech and expression which existed in Eastern Europe before 1989.
3. According to the Chinese government, which right is more important than freedom of speech?
4. True or false?
    Costa Rica is richer than Singapore.
    There is more censorship in Singapore than Japan.
    China and South Africa place many limits on free speech.
5. Give an example from the U.S. of speech constituting a crime.
6. In what ways do France and Britain control expressions of racial antagonism?

Discussion

"Governments should restrict the availability of sex-related material." Write a paragraph containing two arguments for and two against this statement. Then discuss your answer with other students.

17 The rights of citizens

Constitutional law

The previous chapters we considered how the state regulates the behavior of individuals in society by providing rules to be obeyed (criminal law) and procedures for them to solve disputes among each other (civil law). There are also laws which enable citizens to take legal action against the state—against, for example, a public authority or even against the government itself. These actions are part of constitutional law.

Figure 17.1 *The Yanomani Indians pursuing their claim.*

As knowledge of the law has increased among the general public, so have the number and range of constitutional law cases. In 1991, an unmarried couple complained in the Tokyo District Court that it was unconstitutional for the local authority to register their daughter as illegitimate. They said this could lead to discrimination and was against the equality of individuals guaranteed in the Japanese Constitution. Yanomami Indians are pursuing a claim that it is unconstitutional for the Brazilian military to block a 1989 court ruling granting them autonomy over lands in the Amazon rainforest. The military has countered that border security questions must be given priority. In 1976, Gary Gilmore persuaded the U. S. Supreme Court that his death sentence should be carried out since he had been convicted and sentenced for murder according to due legal processes. This brought about a resumption of executions in the United States which continues today.

A **constitution** is the political and ideological structure within which a system of laws operates. Most countries have a formal written Constitution describing how laws are to be made and enforced. The French Constitution, for example, sets a seven year term of office for the president; the U.S. constitution sets a four year term. In Switzerland, a **referendum** (national vote) must be held on any issue for which a petition signed by 10,000 people has been gathered; in Ireland, referenda are to be used only in the case of changes in the constitution itself. In Germany, a change in the constitution requires a special majority vote in parliament, not the simple majority necessary for other laws. Many other countries put the constitution above other laws by making it difficult to change.

Separation of powers

One of the reasons for having special constitutional laws is to prevent governments from becoming too powerful and from interfering too much in the lives of individuals. Whereas socialist legal systems have tended to try to define exactly what the state allowed citizens to do, Anglo-American law has been more concerned with defining what the state could do, arguing that citizens are entitled to do everything other than that which the state forbids. As a check upon overpowerful government most modern constitutions have adopted the principle of separation of powers, developed in the 18th century by the French political philosopher Montesquieu.

Montesquieu argued that the functions of the state could be divided into policy formulation and direction (**executive**), lawmaking (**legislative**), and interpretation and application of the law (**judicial**). To stop governments from becoming too powerful these functions should be carried out by separate institutions, and there should be a balance between them. In the United States, for example, the president (executive) is elected by the people and attempts to carry out his policy promises through a presidential office of advisers. The Constitution gives him many important powers, such as control of the armed forces and appointment of Supreme Court justices, but many of his decisions and all new legislation must be approved by a majority in Congress (legislature), which is also elected by the people. Many presidents have had important policies blocked by Congress. The Supreme Court (judiciary) has the task of interpreting laws which have been disputed in lower courts, and of deciding whether a law passed by Congress or by one of the individual states is in keeping with the Constitution. Recently both pro-choice and anti-abortion groups have organized huge public demonstrations outside the Supreme Court building in the hope of influencing new deliberations about the 1973 abortion legislation.

Rights of citizens

As well as defining the powers of government, most constitutions describe the fundamental rights of citizens. These usually include general declarations about freedom and equality, but also some specific provisions—for instance, the Fifth Amendment of the American Constitution, which exempts a witness from answering a question in court if he states his answer might reveal his own criminal guilt.

Britain is unusual because its constitution is not found in a formal written document. Instead, the constitutional rights of citizens and the powers of government are found in various case-law rulings, statutes, and even in traditions. For example, the important constitutional principle that the king or queen must approve any legislation passed by parliament is simply an unwritten tradition that has gradually developed over the last three hundred years. There is a debate in Britain about whether citizens rights would be better guaranteed by a written constitution, or at least a bill of rights. Some people argue that the government has too much freedom and that it is too easy to change the constitution since all that is needed is a new statute or even a change in traditional procedure. They complain that recent governments have overused libel laws (Chapter 16) and the Official Secrets Act (to censor information in the interests of national security), and feel that citizens' rights have fallen behind those in neighboring European countries will bills of rights. Others argue that the flexibility of an unwritten constitution is a good thing, that the lack of a written constitution has not stood in the way of a long tradition of individual liberty in Britain, and that many countries with constitutions which look liberal on the surface suffer from oppressive governments which simply find ways to ignore constitutional rights.

It can be difficult to compare the legal freedoms of countries with different cultures and economic levels—a problem which will be discussed in the next chapter. But some comparison is possible since many countries have similar constitutional provisions and claim similar aims. We can, for example, consider how effective the provision of separation of powers is. Ferdinand Marcos provides a typical case of overcentralized power; he came to power with wide popular support and many reforming ideas but steadily reduced the rights of Filipino citizens and his family took over most of the executive, legislative and judicial functions of the state.

We can also consider the right of citizens to say and write what they want and to take part in public meetings and demonstrations. In the previous chapter, we compared countries where criticism of the government is virtually forbidden with those where it is freely permitted. Even among the latter there are many differences. In Britain, the 1986 Public Order Act requires advance notice of peaceful protests, even if they do not obstruct other people in any way. In addition, the police may order the protesters to move or break up if they anticipate serious disruption of community life. These laws are more restrictive than those in most European countries, and they are stricter than the pre-1986 laws.

Another area to consider is the ease with which an individual may obtain restitution for a wrong a public body has committed against him. In English law, the principle of **judicial review** enables a court to overturn a decision made a by government ministry that acted illegally or irrationally or beyond its authorized powers. In the 1976 case of Congrieve vs. the Home Office, the British Home Secretary cancelled the television licenses of people who had bought them early to avoid a price increase. Congrieve successfully argued that although the minister had very wide powers to cancel licenses, it was an abuse of his power to do this when nothing illegal had been done.

One important area to consider is the treatment of citizens suspected of crimes. Is innocence presumed unless guilt can be proven? (Yes in Japan and the Philippines, but sometimes no in Taiwan and Malaysia.) How long can the police hold a suspect before they must bring him before a court of law? (Twenty-four hours in Norway, three days and sometimes longer in Finland). Is a suspect entitled to free legal aid and choice of lawyer if he has no money? (Both in New Zealand, only the first in Austria.) Can the police search a private house without first obtaining a court warrant? (Illegal in Argentina, Peru and Paraguay but occasionally done in the first two, and very regularly done in the third.) Are trials open to the public? (Yes in Tanzania and Botswana, often not in Nigeria and Zaire.) Many of these freedoms are so important that they may also be considered in the category of human rights.

The rights of citizens

Exercises

Comprehension
1 Compare the use of referenda in two countries.
2 What is the purpose of separation of powers?
3 True or false?
    a France, Britain and the United States all have constitutions.
    b British citizens are protected by a bill of rights.
    c In Germany and Ireland, it is more difficult to change the constitution than other laws.

Discussion
"It is not constitutions, but politics, that determine citizens' rights."
Write a paragraph containing two arguments for and two against this statement. Then discuss your answer with other students.

18 Human rights

In 1960, Peter Benenson, a British lawyer, read about two students who had been sentenced to seven years' imprisonment for drinking a toast to freedom during the Salazar dictatorship in Portugal. He joined with others to start a campaign for prisoners of conscience—people who had never used or advocated violence and were simply in prison because of their political or religious beliefs. This was the beginning of Amnesty International, the largest of many organizations in the world which put pressure on governments to observe human rights. By gathering information, creating publicity and writing letters, Amnesty has helped to speed up the release of such prisoners all over the world. It also campaigns for fair trials for political prisoners, an end to torture and inhumane treatment, and the abolition of the death penalty. Amnesty and other groups, such as the Anti-Slavery Society and Index on Censorship, have helped make more and more people aware of the concept of human rights—rights that go beyond the laws of one country.

Figure 18.1 *Amnesty International: the human rights organisation.*

Yet, not everyone agrees that merely being born as a human being entitles someone to certain freedoms and treatment, and those who do agree have different opinions as to what these rights are. Many of the rights of citizens mentioned in Chapter 17 are also considered human rights. What needs to be considered here more than the nature of such rights is to whom they apply. A constitutional right is one which a state guarantees to its own citizens and, sometimes, to foreigners who are within its jurisdiction. But a human right is one to which people all over the world are entitled, whatever their nationality and wherever they live.

Law and politics

Most of the law in the world is made by individual governments for their own people. But human rights transcend political divisions. They are basic minimum standards of freedom and security for all. When governments fail to meet these standards, they are criticized by their own citizens, individuals in other countries, and even by foreign governments. Alleging human rights violations, some countries have imposed economic sanctions against others. Many countries have restricted trade to South Africa because of its policy of apartheid. Human rights have been cited as a reason for military intervention against foreign countries—for example, by the Indians in former East Pakistan, the Vietnamese in Cambodia—although there were undoubtedly other reasons for such intervention.

Cultural differences

Is criticism of, and even intervention against, another country justified? There is both a moral and a legal side to this question. Opponents of interference argue that moral standards are the products of different cultures and it is wrong for one culture to impose its values on another. In reply to criticism of its policies in China and Tibet, the Chinese government has repeatedly argued that international human rights organizations make judgments based on the values of Western capitalist nations, and that China has its own values which put more emphasis upon economic security and community solidarity. The governments of some Islamic states have defended the veiling of women and cutting off the hands of thieves as practices founded in their religion and which ensure a safe society. On the legal side, some have argued that the independence of nation states is the basis of the United Nations, the fundamental body of international law and order, and that when one country interferes in the affairs of another it is because its economic and military power, not its human rights policies, is superior.

International agreements

On the other hand, human rights organizations argue that basic moral standards should not depend upon where a person happens to live, especially since many of the governments of the world do not have popular political support among their citizens. Morality and legality become connected when governments violate their own constitutions and when their policies cause citizens to flee over the border into other countries.

Moreover, in purely legal terms, most countries of the world have signed international agreements concerning the treatment of individuals.

Two examples of such agreements are the Universal Declaration of Human Rights (UDHR), adopted by the UN General Assembly in 1948 without a dissenting vote, and the International Covenant on Civil and Political Rights (ICCPR), adopted in 1966. Article 1 of the UDHR declares that all human beings are born free and equal in dignity and rights, and Article Two states that entitlement to rights does not depend upon race, color, sex, language, religion or any other difference among people. Further articles refer to specific rights, such as freedom from slavery (Article 4), torture and cruel punishment (5), and arbitrary arrest and detention (9); the right to a fair, independent and public hearing of a criminal charge (10); the right to own property and to choose employment (17.23); and the right to express one's opinions (19) and to take part peacefully in assemblies (20). The 1966 ICCPR is not as comprehensive as the UNHR 1948, but is more important because it carries the force of a treaty obligation. Among other things it has provisions about racial and sexual equality (2); torture and slavery (7 and 8); freedom of movement (12); and freedom of thought, conscience and religion (17). However, only half of the members of the United Nations have so far signed the Convention, and only 34 countries have agreed to an Optional Protocol which allows individuals to seek redress in a court of law against violations of the Convention.

The European Convention on Human Rights (ECHR) was first adopted in 1950 and has now been signed by every country of Western Europe. Individual citizens of these countries have the right to bring a complaint before the European Commission if they think their government has broken the Convention. If the Commission agrees, it may try to persuade the country in question to rectify the breach, or it may refer the matter to the European Court of Human Rights, which has the right to order a change of law in that country. Covering countries with similar cultures and economic conditions, the ECHR is more practical than many international human rights agreements. However, individual governments still manage to delay making changes to their laws by claiming special national interests.

When the laws of a country violate human rights, groups like Amnesty International protest to the government on moral grounds. But whenever possible, legal arguments are also used—references to the constitution of the country itself and to any relevant international agreements which its government has signed. But despite the development of legally binding national and international conventions, millions of people in the world still do not enjoy human rights.

Human rights violations

In 1978, Saida Botan Elmi was arrested by the Somali government. She was held in prison for six years and frequently tortured. Torture is defined in the 1949 Geneva Convention, as "the deliberate, systematic or wanton infliction of physical and mental suffering." Sometimes it is used to extract information from prisoners, and sometimes it is used for no other reason than to hurt and frighten them. The use of torture violates international human rights laws, no matter what crime a prisoner has committed. In the case of Saida Botan Elmi, her only crime was to want to join her husband, who had resigned as a judge and left Somalia rather than implement laws that he believed were unfair. She was adopted as a prisoner of conscience by Amnesty International.

In 1982, Saul Godinez Cruz disappeared in Honduras after leaving home for work. Someone saw a military officer take him away, but he was never seen again. The government never acknowledged his arrest or detention. Between 1980 and 1988, the United Nations investigated over 15,000 similar disappearances in 40 countries. Governments sometimes kill civilians because of their political beliefs, race, or even because they were in the wrong place at the wrong time; they then cover up any information about the killing in order to avoid responsibility. In the case of Saul Godinez Cruz, the Inter-American Court of Human Rights held, in 1989, that the government of Honduras was in breach of the UDHR and should pay his family compensation of $75,000.

In 1973, Shabaka WaQlimi tried to rob a bank in Florida, gave up, and the next day gave himself up to the police. But he was charged with the murder of an attorney's wife, which he knew nothing about. His robbery accomplice gave false evidence against him to avoid prosecution himself. In addition, one member of the all-white jury is reported to have made racist remarks during the trial. Mr. WaQlimi was sentenced to death and spent over thirteen years on a prison death row before the truth of his innocence finally emerged. Human rights groups work to ensure that all trials are fair: that judges and juries are independent and unbiased; that suspects have access to adequate legal advice; and that prisoners are not held in jail for too long before a trial takes place. Amnesty has received reports of people held in Syrian prisons for eighteen years without ever having a trial. In the case of trials of political prisoners, Amnesty insists that they be held in public and that observers from independent countries be allowed to observe the proceedings.

A very large area of human rights law is concerned with refugees. Over fifteen million people have fled from their own countries because of human rights abuses, political pressures or economic hardship, they need international guarantees that they will be treated fairly and humanely in foreign countries. Many are seeking **political asylum**—the right to live in a new country—because of fears of what will happen to them if they are returned. In 1987, Sri Lankan refugees organized a dramatic demonstration at Heathrow airport, claiming that British immigration authorities gave them no opportunity to explain why they were seeking asylum and no access to legal representation. Many Rohingas refugees who fled to Bangladesh in 1991 have been threatened with forcible return to Myanmar.

As human rights issues grow, they provoke more and more debate. Is freedom from economic hardship, as many socialist countries claim, the most important right? Are economic refugees, as some of the Vietnamese in camps in Hong Kong appear to be, entitled to asylum in a foreign country? Is the death penalty, as Amnesty has argued since 1977, always a violation of human rights? What about the right not to be sentenced to corporal (physical) punishment? The right to practice one's religion in a public place? The right to have a homosexual relationship? The right to medical treatment?

Racial and sexual discrimination

Few people would disagree with the right to racial equality, but what about sexual equality? In 1990, a group of women in Saudi Arabia deliberately broke the law by driving cars in a country where only men are permitted to drive. They were arrested and only released from prison when male members of their family promised to "keep them out of trouble." Political and legal discrimination against women includes lesser voting rights (in parts of Switzerland); official discouragement from entering politics (Singapore); and the need for a wife to get her husband's consent when she applies for a passport (Egypt). In Japan, where only seven of the nation's 1,257 detention centers have any female guards, there have been reports of women being strip searched even for traffic offences. Many women are arrested in Japan are illegal foreign workers, and this makes it less likely that their human rights will be observed. Women also suffer economic and social inequality throughout the world, either doing less well-paid work than men or being paid less for doing the same work. In addition, they are underrepresented in parliaments and on boards of directors. There is debate about how much legal reform can actually help solve social problems like these.

Exercises

Comprehension
1 Describe four of Amnesty International's aims.
2 Mention one argument for, and one against, intervention against another country because of its human rights policies.
3 Name three international agreements on human rights.
4 True or false? Amnesty supports its criticisms with
   a legal arguments.
   b moral arguments.
   c political arguments.
5 List five ways in which women in some countries appear to suffer unfair treatment.

Discussion
"Matters such as corporal punishment and the status of women should be left up to individual societies, not international organizations."
Write a paragraph containing two arguments for and two against this statement. Then discuss your answer with other students.

19 Enforcing the law

Governments have many ways of making sure that citizens obey the law. They make the public aware of what the law is and try to encourage social support for law and order. They use police forces to investigate crimes and catch criminals. They authorize courts to complete the investigation of criminal and civil offences and to pass sentences to punish the guilty and deter others. And they make efforts to re-educate and reform people who have broken the law. Which of these is most effective in enforcing the law?

The laws of all countries are to be found in written records—the legal codes of countries with continental systems, the statutes and case judgments of common law countries, warnings on official forms, and notices in public buildings. Many people do not know where to find these records and do not find it easy to read them. But ignorance of the law is almost never a defence for breaking it. Governments usually expect citizens to be aware of the laws which affect their lives. Sometimes this seems very harsh, for example, when the law is very technical. Shopkeepers in England have been prosecuted for selling books on Sunday, although they were allowed to sell magazines. However, there are many laws, such as those prohibiting theft, assault and dangerous driving, which simply reflect social and moral attitudes to everyday behavior. In such cases a person knows he is breaking the law, even if he doesn't know exactly which law it is.

Role of police force

The police have many functions in the legal process. Though they are mainly concerned with criminal law, they may also be used to enforce judgments made in civil courts (see Chapter 3). As well as gathering information for offences to be prosecuted in the courts, the police have wide powers to arrest, search and question people suspected of crimes and to control the actions of members of the public during public demonstrations and assemblies. In some countries, the police have judicial functions; for example, they may make a decision as to guilt in a driving offense and impose a fine, without the involvement of a court. In Britain, when someone is found in possession of marijuana, the police may confiscate it and issue a formal warning rather than refer the matter to a court.

The mere presence of the police is a factor in deterring people from committing offences. In Japan, you are rarely more than a ten-minute walk from a small police station. The city of Tokyo has more policemen than the city of New York. Could this be one reason there is less crime in Japan than

Enforcing the law

the United States? Comparing the crime figures of different countries is a complex matter. It is necessary to consider not only how many crimes are committed, but how many are detected and recorded. In 1989, over 13,000 offenses were reported in both New Zealand and Sweden for every 100,000 people, compared with less than 200 in Brazil and Argentina, but this does not necessarily mean that South Americans are 650 times more law-abiding. The type of crime is another important factor. Britain has more reported crime in general than Japan but about the same number of murders (1.5 per 100,000 people, compared with 8.6 in the United States and 29 in the Bahamas). Rich countries tend to have more car thefts than poor ones.

Figure 19.1 *The smiling face of law enforcement.*

A just legal system needs an independent, honest police force. In countries where the public trusts the police force, they are more likely to report crimes, and it seems that they are also more likely to be law-abiding. Because of their wide powers it would not be difficult for corrupt police forces to falsify evidence against a suspect, to mistreat someone they have arrested, or to accept bribes in return for overlooking offences. In 1991, the Osaka High Court ordered the review of a Hong Kong man's case after finding that the police had used a biased interpreter. In 1991, the Japanese Civil Liberties Union believes there have been numerous case of police violence against foreign suspects, many of who are not told of their rights in a language which they can understand. In the Birmingham Six case, British police officers obtained confessions from men suspected of bombing a pub by beating them up. In the United States, illegally obtained evidence is not valid in court, but in Britain the court decides whether it is fair to accept such evidence on a case-by-case basis. A confession obtained by force would not be allowed, but one obtained by trickery might.

Legal systems usually have codes of conduct for the police, limiting the time and the methods which they can use to question suspects and guaranteeing the suspects access to independent lawyers. In Britain, however, the Police and Criminal Evidence Act, and especially the Prevention of Terrorism Act, give the police some powers to delay access to lawyers. The Police Complaints Authority was set up in 1984 to supervise the investigation of allegations of police misconduct. No police officer or former police officer may be appointed to the authority. However, investigations themselves are carried out by police officers. Of course, private legal action can be taken against a police officer as against any other individual—for example, in the tort of false imprisonment. But many people feel it is difficult to gather evidence against the police.

In some countries, police officers are usually armed, whereas in others they only carry guns when engaged in certain kinds of work. Governments may also make use of the army to enforce the law, but this is only done on a regular basis when there is political dissatisfaction with the government, either from a large part of the civilian population (Paraguay), or from a well-armed minority (Northern Ireland). Since armies are trained for wartime conditions, their methods of law enforcement are unlikely to be completely impartial, although there are some countries where the army appears to enjoy more public confidence than the police (India).

The court system was discussed in Chapter 4. As with the police, it is important that the public feels the judiciary is independent and unbiased. Americans feel that the best way of ensuring this is to have elected judges. Britons fear this might lead to politicalization of the judiciary and prefer to have judges appointed by the government on the recommendation of the lord chancellor.

Although courts have the highest legal authority, they rely on the power of the prison authorities to enforce their decisions. They can authorize the detention of an individual in order to gather evidence against him, compel him to obey a court order or punish him for a crime.

Civil and criminal penalties

There are several kinds of punishment available to the courts. In civil cases, the most common punishment is a fine, but specific performance and injunctions may also be ordered (see Chapters 2 and 3). For criminal offenses fines are also often used when the offense is not a very serious one and when the offender has not been in trouble before. Another kind of punishment available in some countries is **community service**. This requires the offender to do a certain amount of unpaid work, usually for a social institution such as a hospital. For more serious crimes the usual punishment is imprisonment. Some prison sentences are **suspended**: the offender is not sent to prison if he keeps out of trouble for a fixed period of time, but if he does offend again both the suspended sentence and any new one will be imposed. The length of sentences varies from a few days to a lifetime. However, a life sentence may allow the prisoner to be released after a suitably long period if a review (parole) board agrees his detention no longer serves a purpose. In some countries, such as the Netherlands, living conditions in prison are fairly good because it is felt that deprivation of liberty is punishment in itself and should not be so harsh that it reduces the possibility of the criminal re-educating and reforming himself. In other countries, conditions are very bad. Perhaps because of an increase in crime or because of more and longer sentences of imprisonment, some prison cells have to accommodate far more people than they were built to hold and the prisoners are only let out of their cells once a day. Britain and the United States are trying to solve the shortage of space by allowing private companies to open prisons.

In some countries there is also **corporal punishment** (physical). In Malaysia, Singapore, Pakistan, Zambia, Zimbabwe, among others, courts may sentence offenders to be caned or whipped. In Saudi Arabia theft and possession of alcohol may be punished by cutting off the offender's hand or foot.

Capital punishment

The ultimate penalty is death (**capital punishment**). It is carried out by hanging (Kenya, for example); electrocution, gassing or lethal injection (U.S.); beheading or stoning (Saudi Arabia); or shooting (China). Although most countries still have a death penalty, 35 (including almost every European nation) have abolished it; 18 retain it only for exceptional crimes such as wartime offences; and 27 no longer carry out executions even when a death sentence has been passed. In other words, almost half the countries of the world have ceased to use the death penalty. The UN has declared itself in favor of abolition, Amnesty International actively campaigns for abolition, and the issue is now the focus of great debate.

Supporters of capital punishment believe that death is a just punishment for certain serious crimes. Many also believe that it deters others from committing such crimes. Opponents argue that execution is cruel and uncivilized. Capital punishment involves not only the pain of dying (James Autry took ten minutes to die of lethal injection in Texas, 1984) but also the mental anguish of waiting, sometimes for years, to know if and when the sentence will be carried out. Opponents also argue that there is no evidence that it deters people from committing murder any more than imprisonment does. A further argument is that, should a mistake be made, it is too late to rectify it once the execution has taken place. In 1987, two academics published a study showing that 23 innocent people had been executed in the United States. Research has shown that capital punishment is used inconsistently. For example, in South Africa, black murderers are far more likely to be sentenced to death than whites. During a crime wave in China in the 1980s, cities were given a quota of executions to meet; in a city where there weren't very many murders, people convicted of lesser crimes were more likely to be executed. In addition, while in some countries young people are not sent to prison but to special juvenile detention centres, in Nigeria, Iran, Iraq, Bangladesh, Barbados and the United States children under 18 have been legally put to death.

As the debate about capital punishment continues, the phenomenon of **death row** (people sentenced but still alive) increases. In 1991, no one was executed in Japan, but three people were sentenced to death, bringing the total number on death row to fifty. Sakae Menda lived under sentence of death for thirty three years before obtaining a retrial and being found not guilty. The debate also involves the question of what punishment is for. Is the main aim to deter? This was certainly the case in 18th century England when the penalty for theft was supposed to frighten people from stealing and compensate for inabilities to detect and catch thieves. Is it revenge or retribution? Is it to keep criminals out of society? Or is it to reform and rehabilitate them?

Enforcing the law

Exercises

Comprehension

1. List as many functions of the police as you can think of.
2. Why do crime figures not necessarily give an accurate picture of the amount of crime in a country?
3. True or false?
   a. In Britain, complaints against the police are investigated by police officers themselves.
   b. American judges are elected.
   c. Most countries still retain the death penalty.
4. What is parole?

Discussion

"Imprisonment is revenge, but not rehabilitation."

Write a paragraph containing two arguments for and two against this statement. Then discuss your answer with other students.

20 Internationalization of the law

In the first chapter of this book we discussed the fact that most laws are the creation of individual nations. Yet it has also been argued that many countries face similar social, economic and political problems and consequently have adopted similar legal solutions. Some areas of the law, such as intellectual property and human rights, are particularly concerned with developing laws which are valid internationally. With more international business and travel and a growing awareness that many socio-economic and environment problems need global solutions, the future of the world of law appears to be one of internationalization.

There are two main kinds of international law: private and public. The former concerns the role of foreign laws within a particular country. For example, if an Englishman wants to sell property he owns in France to another Englishman, any English court must consider French law when deciding the legality of the contract of sale. Public international law, on the other hand, deals with relations between states.

Growth of international law

International law is not new. Nations have always made political and economic treaties with each other. In Medieval Europe, the Canon Law of the Catholic Church had an important role. Law Merchant regulated trade across political frontiers. In the fifteenth century, the Church mediated rivalry between Spain and Portugal by dividing the world into their respective areas of interest. The 1648 Treaty of Westphalia, which called for equal treatment everywhere of Protestants and Catholics, can be seen as an early international human rights law. Nevertheless, most international law has been created in the twentieth century. The League of Nations was set up after World War I to regulate disputes between nations. However, it failed to stop the tension that led to World War II, partly because some powerful countries did not join (U.S.) and others left when they disagreed with its decisions (Germany, Japan). But it led to important international legislation like the Geneva Convention on the treatment of prisoners of war and the 1951 Convention on the Status of Refugees.

There are some important differences between international laws and those created inside individual states. Domestic laws are passed by legislative bodies, most of which have some popular political support. International laws, on the other hand, are created by agreements among governments. As a result, it is not as clear whether they have the support of individual citizens. Enforcement of international law is also different. Many international agreements are not binding—for example, UN General Resolutions. Even when nations agree to be bound, as in the case of the signatories of the 1966 International Convention on Civil and Political Rights, it is unclear how obligations are to be enforced. At certain times particular nations have acted like a police force. Since the 1991 Gulf War, the U.S.-dominated international peacekeeping operation has perhaps come nearer to playing this role of world police force than anyone previously, having more military power than former UN peacekeeping forces and being prepared to use it. But the operation's temporary nature and self-interested motives mean it differs from a true police force.

The end of Cold War tension and the 1991 Gulf War seem to have produced a new consensus in the world about international war. One of the basic principles of the UN Charter was that one nation should not interfere in the internal affairs of another. But Resolution 688, passed by the UN Security Council on April 5, 1991, ordered Iraq to grant access to international humanitarian organizations so that assistance could be given to refugees, and authorized military action against Iraq if access were refused. The right to interfere seems to be replacing the principle of non-intervention, but there is great debate about just when such interference is acceptable. (This is more of a political issue than a legal one.)

In the 1979 case of Marckx, representatives of an illegitimate Belgian obtained a ruling from the Court of the European Convention of Human Rights that laws favoring the children of married couples in Belgium were discriminatory. In the Brogan case of 1985 a man held in Britain for four days before being brought before a court, obtained a ruling from the same court that the Prevention of Terrorism Act under which he had been held was in violation of the European Convention. However, Britain has avoided changing this law by arguing that the Convention gives exemption where a country's vital interests are at stake.

Conflicts of national sovereignty

The European Community has provided many interesting cases in the development of international law. Starting as a series of economic agreements between six nations in the 1950s, Community Law now has direct authority in the social and economic affairs of twelve countries. In theory, each member state has agreed to be bound by EC decisions. So what happens when the laws of one country directly conflict with those of the Community?

A year before Britain joined the European Community in 1973, the respected judge Lord Denning suggested that membership would reduce

Internationalization of the law

Figure 20.1 *There is a growing need for international law in areas like environmental pollution.*

the **sovereignty** (independent power) of the British parliament. But in 1979 he said that British courts would have to follow all British laws, even ones that conflicted with Community law. When an internal law has conflicted with European law there has usually been some modification of internal law. But what would happen if the conflict could not be resolved? Is each member country free to continue to do as it chooses or to leave the Community? Some people argue that the 1972 European Communities act (by which Britain entered the EC) is like any other law passed by the British parliament and can therefore be repealed. But others argue that by passing the 1972 act, parliament accepted a new legal order which reduced its powers. If this is so, Britain could not legally disobey a European ruling, or even leave the EC, without the consent of other member nations.

The European Community has provided a great deal of work for lawyers. The number of Europeans entering the legal profession has been increasing, but the demand for lawyers has increased even faster, especially for those who can speak another language. However, although the movement of labor among European countries has increased a great deal, there are still many restrictions upon the legal profession. An English lawyer, for example, may work in France under the title of "solicitor," but he may not do the same work as a French "conseil juridique" unless he passes French law examinations.

Internationalizing legal systems

The internationalization of the Japanese legal system has even further to go. Foreign lawyers may be employed in Japanese law companies, but they are not allowed to work on cases that involve Japanese laws, or to run law firms in partnership with Japanese lawyers. It seems there is nothing to stop them from taking the Japanese law examinations, but these are almost impossible to pass for anyone who is not a native speaker of Japanese.

Continuing differences among legal systems seem to be a major barrier to the internationalization of the legal profession. Nevertheless such barriers are breaking down. International business requires contracts that are internationally valid and lawyers who can argue cases in the courts of different countries. The number of international tort cases is increasing. For example in 1981, workers injured in an American-owned Union Carbide factory in Bhopal, India, took their case to the United States. When political circumstances allow, individuals take legal action to force their government to obey international agreements, and every year such agreements increase. The 1990s have seen old states disappear (for example, the Soviet Union) and new ones appear (Slovenia). At the same time, civil wars, refugee crises and environmental disasters are demonstrating the need for more laws across frontiers.

Since the UN is not a world government but a conference of the world's existing national governments, the limitations of international law become clear whenever there is a dispute between a nation and an ethnic group within its borders. Without a national government, the Tibetans (ruled by China and the Kurds (spread across Iraq, Turkey and Syria) face enormous difficulties in publicizing their social and economic problems. The admission of the Koreas and the former Soviet and Yugoslav republics to the UN has helped to make the organization more representative. However, the increasing tendency of states in Eastern Europe and the Caucasus to fragment into ethnic factions suggests that there will never be enough nations to represent all the citizens of the world. The concept of world citizens directly electing a world government still seems remote. But there are signs that the fundamental rights of national governments are being questioned. In September 1992 the UN made history by expelling a member state—Yugoslavia.

While movement toward an international government continues to be slow, international law is developing rapidly in the form of limited practical agreements to facilitate trade and protect the environment. More and more people are affected by activities in areas that are not under the exclusive control of any one nation. Pilots and air traffic controllers work within guidelines laid down by the 1944 Chicago Convention, when traffic was only a fraction of its present volume. Homeowners can turn to the 1972 Convention on International Liability for Damage Caused by Space Objects when space debris falls on their property (as happened to Canadians in 1979). Even Antarctica and outer space are subject to several pieces of legislation to prevent them becoming as dirty and dangerous as the rest of the world.

As fast as international law grows, it is not fast enough. Conventions on Environmental Protection in Geneva (1979), Vienna (1985) and Rio (1992) have managed to emphasize not only the seriousness of the problems but the political and economic difficulties of doing anything about them. The 1982 Law of the Sea builds upon some of the oldest international law in the world, covering such matters as rights of passage through straits, deep-sea mining, the rights of landlocked states, piracy and collisons. But the number of disputes, hijackings and accidents gets more, not less. The future of law, the "necessary evil," seems to be one of inevitable expansion.

Exercises

Comprehension
1. Mention three pre-20th century forms of international law.
2. Describe two differences between international and domestic law.
3. List three growing areas of international law.

Discussion
What do you think is the international problem which would most benefit from greater internationalization of the law? Write a paragraph giving reasons, then discuss this with other students.

Glossary

Appeal A request to a higher court to re-examine and change the judgment of a previous court hearing.

Appellant The party that requests an **Appeal**.

Articled clerk Someone who has passed the examination to become a **Solicitor** but is receiving training from another solicitor so that he or she can become qualified.

Bail Allowing a person who has been charged with a crime to remain free (outside **Custody**) until the date of the next court hearing. Bail may be **Conditional**, in which case the person is only allowed to remain free so long as he or she fulfills certain conditions, such as guaranteeing a sum of money or giving up his passport. If there are no such conditions it is called **Unconditional bail**.

Barrister A lawyer who specializes in arguing on behalf of the **Defendant**, the **Plaintiff**, or the **Prosecution**, in court.

Censor To examine, change, and sometimes ban an item of news, literature or art before it is available to the public.

Civil law Those areas of law in which both parties are usually private citizens or companies.

Contract An agreement between two or more people which is binding in law. If one party fails to fulfill his obligations under the agreement it is called **Breach of Contract**.

Common law A system in which legal decisions are based upon decisions in previous cases (see **Doctrine of precedent**) and on custom, rather than on detailed written laws. It is sometimes called case law and originally developed in England. Common law is an important part of the legal systems of many countries which have been influenced by English law, such as the USA and India.

Continental law A system in which legal decisions are usually made by applying detailed written laws to the case in question. Various forms of continental law are found in continental Europe and in parts of Asia, Africa and Latin America. It is sometimes known as **Roman law** because it was influenced by the laws developed in ancient Rome. It is also sometimes known as codified law because the system often requires laws to be written in the form of precise, detailed codes.

Custody   (i) Being held at a police station or in prison.
(ii) The right to care for a child and to have him or her live with you.

Damages Money paid by one party of a legal action (usually civil) to compensate the other party for loss or injury.

Defamation The **Tort** of saying or writing something which is untrue and which harms another person's good name.

Defendant The party that is accused in court of a crime or a civil offense.

Glossary

Doctrine of precedent The practice of making legal decisions by following the decision made in a previous similar case. If there is no previous similar case the court will decide by applying existing laws to a new set of facts and its decision will become a new precedent for courts to follow in the future.

Equity The ordinary meaning is *justice* or *fairness*, but the word also covers a system of law developed in England and other **Common law** countries to supplement the existing law where it seemed inadequate or unfair. The common law and equitable systems have now merged.

Judicial review The right to ask a court to re-examine and sometimes cancel an act of a government institution or another court of law on the grounds that it is unconstitutional.

Jury A group of ordinary men or women without special legal training who are selected to hear evidence in court and then decide whether the defendant is guilty or not.

Jury service The duty to attend court for a limited period of time and without payment as a member of a Jury.

Plaintiff The party that starts or carries out civil proceedings. It is usually a private citizen or company.

Prosecution The party that starts or carries out criminal proceedings in court. It is often a lawyer employed by the state, or the police themselves.

Public law Those areas of law which involve the state as one of the parties to an action. The main branches are Criminal law, Constitutional law, and International law.

Punitive damages A court order that the loser of a civil action pay to the winner a sum of money (**Damages**) so great that it will be a warning not to repeat the wrongdoing.

Pupil Someone who has passed the examination to become a **Barrister** but is receiving training so that he or she can become fully qualified.

Roman Law A tradition of law developed in ancient Rome which has influenced and been expanded upon by many countries which have a **Continental** system of law.

Solicitor A lawyer whose main job is to advise clients and prepare cases before a court hearing takes place.

Strict liability Legal responsibility for a crime or civil wrongdoing even when no fault or knowledge of the wrongdoing can be shown.

Tort A wrongdoing for which a private citizen (or company) is sued by another private citizen.

Treason The crime of betraying (being disloyal) or endangering the government of the country in which you live or work.